PENGUIN BOOKS
THE JOY OF VEGETARIAN COOKING

Jasleen Dhamija has been closely involved with the development
of textiles, folk arts and crafts. In 1954 she started working with
the Handicrafts Board and for the next seventeen years was
involved in the revival of crafts, and in community development
and women's employment. It was while she was working for the
UN in Iran (1970-77) that she became closely involved with the
revival of traditional art forms. From 1978 to 1982 Jasleen
headed the Pan-African Centre for Development of Small
Industries and Crafts. Since 1994 she has been working in Central
Asia for the revival of the Silk Route.

Jasleen has been the Hill Visiting Professor, University of
Minnesota, Resident Fellow at Canberra School of Art, and has
been on the Creative Arts Faculty at the University of
Wallongong, and Sydney College of Arts in Australia. She has
written over a dozen books on crafts, textiles and living cultural
traditions. During her extensive travels she has sampled different
cuisines, collected innumerable recipes and improvised them to
her taste. She combines her passion for food with an abiding
interest in Ayurveda. For the last ten years she has concentrated
on evolving recipes for healthy eating based on the Ayurvedic
system. *The Joy of Vegetarian Cooking* is a direct result of this.

THE JOY OF
VEGETARIAN
COOKING

Jasleen Dhamija

PENGUIN BOOKS

An imprint of Penguin Random House

PENGUIN BOOKS

USA | Canada | UK | Ireland | Australia
New Zealand | India | South Africa | China | Singapore

Penguin Books is part of the Penguin Random House group of companies
whose addresses can be found at global.penguinrandomhouse.com

Published by Penguin Random House India Pvt. Ltd
4th Floor, Capital Tower 1, MG Road,
Gurugram 122 002, Haryana, India

Penguin
Random House
India

First published by Penguin Books India 2000

Illustrations by Roma Sinai Mukherjee

10 9 8 7 6 5 4

ISBN 9780140287493

Typeset in Sabon by Digital Technologies and Printing Solutions, New Delhi

Printed at Manipal Technologies Limited, India

www.penguin.co.in

MIX
Paper | Supporting
responsible forestry
FSC® C043100

This book is dedicated to Ishwar Sharma, friend and healer, who insisted that I should write down the recipes so that they would make his diet more acceptable to his patients

&

Peter Lawton, my dear brother-in-law, who encouraged me to finish the book when I had given it up.

Contents

F o r e w o r d

Jasleen Dhamija is a remarkable person. Along with her complete involvement and dedication to craft from the early age of twenty, she has been extremely interested in food as an expression of the ethos of a people.

Her work in traditional crafts has taken Jasleen all over rural India. She has also travelled extensively in Africa, Iran, Iraq, Central Asia, Australia and America. Her travels have enabled her to sample and appreciate different cuisines, experiment with them and then to innovate. In her book she has given recipes from all over the world as well as some delightful innovations of her own.

Her first book on folk arts and crafts of India, published in 1970, ran to seven editions. This book, I am sure, will do the same because though she is so involved in the numerous aspects of craft, which is a lifetime of work, she also has a passion for food and is only too aware of its importance to mankind.

Among other things, Jasleen is involved in many UNESCO projects and was appointed the President of the Jury for UNESCO Asian Prize for Creativity 1991 and she continues in that capacity till today.

Her interest in Ayurvedic forms of health food came from her contact with Dr Ishwar Sharma, who comes from a renowned family of Vaids and influenced her deeply. Most of Jasleen's recipes reflect her health consciousness.

I wish her every success in her new venture on vegetarian cooking.

Bhicoo J. Manekshaw   New Delhi
February 2000

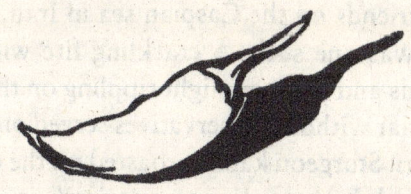

An Introduction to Jasleen's Rasoi

In 1978, when I was on my way to Ethiopia, if I had been asked whom I would choose to be with if shipwrecked, I would have said without hesitation: My cook, any day!

I had just heard that my application for a visa for my cook to accompany me to Ethiopia had been rejected. I, who love to eat, had no clue about how to cook. My knowledge was limited to tastes and flavours. I loved to explore different textures, combinations and aromas of different cuisines. I have always felt a country's culture is reflected in its cuisine. My most memorable experiences have come from a combination of good company, beautiful location and delicious food. The fantastic picnic with Persian friends on the Caspian sea in Iran, on a full moon night, was one such. A crackling fire with sparks rising skywards and the moonlight rippling on the waters, with fresh caviar without preservatives served on buttered *naan-e-barbari*. Sturgeon kababs roasted on the open fire, served with fresh herbs and *naan-e-sangark*, is a memory forever etched not only in my mind, but in my olfactory senses.

I remember a picnic on the road to Bodrum in Turkey, when we stopped at a remote Greek site, after criss-crossing the river Meander. Large pillars stood erect, silent witnesses to the passage of time. As we walked, we crushed marjoram and rosemary leaves under our feet and their fragrance filled the air. We plucked wild herbs for our picnic and the upturned faces of old Greek statues stared at us, their eyes moistened with dew. We leaned against fluted Greek pillars while seated on beautiful hand-woven Anatolian *jajim* and unpacked our picnic basket of local dried black olives delicately flavoured with herbs, goat cheese encased in skin, pickled vegetables and slices of pasterma, eaten with fresh crusty local bread. We swigged from a bottle of local wine, which we had chilled in the stream nearby, and finished our picnic by nibbling at fist-sized figs, sweet and succulent.

My childhood memories are of picnics, the only form of outings that we had in our small town in the North West Frontier Province. We celebrated the first snowfall by climbing the *Cheera-walli-Pahari* (pine-covered hill), our pockets stuffed with lumps of jaggery enriched with walnuts, black cumin, raisins and almonds, which came from Peshawar. We nibbled at the jaggery and bit into fresh snow, the combination being the only version of ice cream that we could get.

Basant Panchami, the spring festival when everyone wore yellow to match the colour of the sprouting mustard flowers, was a day for an extended family picnic. Boys flew kites of myriad colours, while girls were restricted to just holding the reel of thread. Women cooked cauldrons full of aromatic dishes, the fragrance of the herbs mingling with wood smoke and the scent of pine needles.

In summer, picnics were organized when cousins living in Delhi and Lahore visited us. They were the city people who came in their cars and together we drove to the Jandars, a place of flowing water, dams and water mills. While we tasted chocolates, biscuits and other goodies brought from the big cities, these cousins and aunts raved about wild black mushroom, morrel which we called *guchi*, and pulao with raisins.

I never learnt to cook and the more often I was asked what I would feed my husband without culinary skills, the greater became my resolve never to be in a position where I would have to cook. I learnt to reply to such remarks quite early with: I'll marry a man who knows how to cook. 'Well, Well!' Granny would say, 'he will have to be an angrez, only they can be henpecked into cooking!'

I developed a mental block about cooking. In fact, I could not even light a fire, for in those days there were no gas and electric cookers; one cooked on wood or on coal. Later kerosene stoves came into use, but even those I never mastered. I had a mortal fear of the pressure stove. Having once set the kitchen on fire, no one asked me to enter it again. Luckily, I was always able to afford a cook, so there was no problem. Later, when I travelled, my cook accompanied me. Believe it or not, when I went trekking in the mountains, he came trekking too, valiantly marching ahead to rouse the chowkidar to get the rest house opened and commandeer the kitchen.

When I went to work in Iran, my cook went with me. I always loved reading cookbooks and worked with my cook to devise new recipes. But everytime I tried my hand at cooking, it was a disaster. The food either got charred or became abysmally mushy. My friend, Carmen Kagal, was still worse and managed to burn even her dog's food. She even burnt her own bandages and plastic eye cup while trying to sterilize them.

Despite valiant efforts I had failed to get a visa for my cook to join me in Addis Ababa so I had no choice but to learn how to cook or eat the nondescript food of the dreadful restaurants or the wishy-washy cooking of the English-speaking Ethiopian cooks, who prided themselves on having perfected the art of English cuisine. When asked to cook Ethiopian food, which was very similar to Indian food, the stock reply was, 'My wife only cook. Me, I specialist of cooking English.'

I finally accepted defeat, swallowed my pride and flew down to Nairobi, since Addis Ababa had no decent bookshops, and bought a few cookbooks. With Madhur Jaffrey's *An Invitation to Indian Cooking*, the *Joy of Cooking* and the *All Asian CookBook*, I smugly returned to embark on my cooking career. My first couple of meals were a disaster.

It was because of my son, Himman, that I made a real effort to learn cooking. He was to come from boarding school, starved for edible food, and I wanted to make the effort to produce something nice for him. So evenings were spent with him poring over cookbooks, choosing the simplest recipes for starters. My attempts were disastrous and I would weep tears of frustration. Himman would console me gently, saying: 'Mamma, they are not bad, see we put a little tabasco, squeeze a little lime and cut away the charred pieces and then they are fine.' Slowly the first edible meals began to happen, for which I really owe my thanks to Madhur Jaffrey's book. I remembered the petite Madhur Bahadur with thanks, as I religiously followed each comma, each mark, in her book. I then regretted our rather acrimonious election campaign at Miranda House, when we both stood for the college presidentship.

At the end of six months I felt confident enough to start experimenting with cooking, so all the cookbooks were banished. I would go to the markets in Addis Ababa and come back with all kinds of ingredients, much to the surprise of my colleagues and Ethiopian friends. They found fermented *kocho* from the false bananas in my refrigerator, which I cooked mixed with Indian spices and wrapped in banana leaves. I prepared my own soup for the delicious *fitt-fitt* made of crushed and dried *injera*, their local bread. Every trip I made to another country, I learnt a new dish and came back with new ingredients like *harissa*, the red chilli paste from Tunisia, the dried *fufu* from Ghana, and of course, dried fruits and dried herbs, to create my favourite dishes from Iran and Turkey.

New York, which I visited once a year from Africa, became my favourite food place. I met a number of gourmets there, who had a passion for different cuisines. Everything was available. I could get the *panch poron* of Bengal, the *kokam* of the West Coast, the *kasuri methi* of the North, the *besan* for *kadhi* and *khandvi*, and coconut cream and grated coconut, from the Indian grocers. The Lebanese shops sold dried *sabzi*—herbs used in the preparation of pulao, *leemu ommani* or dried lime, *kashk* or dried yoghurt, *paneer-eh khushk* of Tabriz, *albalu khushk*, and dried *talkhun*. Besides, there was the added convenience of getting everything clean and ready to use. A number of ingredients which otherwise took hours to prepare were readily available in processed packages. When I returned from New York, my clothes were in my hand baggage and all the goodies in the suitcase.

In New York, one could buy frozen vegetables all cleaned and prepared for cooking. Thanks to the Vietnamese, there were fresh fruits and vegetables all cut and ready. The fish and meat shops were wonderful, with prepared prawns shelled and deveined, fillet of fish ready for cooking, roasts prepared for the oven, and dressed chicken. Life was so easy and wonderful. I slowly perfected the art of getting a four-course meal ready in forty-five minutes, much to the amazement of friends who had known me in my previous avatar when I couldn't even make a cup of tea, except when it was all brewed and put in front of me. I would then do the memsahib bit: How would you like your tea? Do have these cucumber sandwiches with a touch of garlic chutney!

However, it was only when I came back home in 1988 and was introduced to naturopathy by my friend and doctor Ishwar Sharma, that I developed a cuisine which I think is special. It is delicious, rich in the aroma of many cultures, yet healthy. I was then constantly suffering from all kinds of ailments, my energy level was low and life lacked excitement. I used to grouch with a friend of mine, who complained of migraine, pain, lingering cough and cold, but when I met her after a gap of three months, she was five kilos slimmer, her face was bright, even her voice had changed. I asked her how this miracle had happened and she introduced me to Dr Ishwar Sharma.

Ishwar, as I call him, is a man of many interests. He specialized in yoga, worked with the naturopathy centre in Bangalore and studied reflexology which he practises. He comes from a traditional family of Vaids who practised Ayurveda. Ishwar has a wonderful sense of humour and is very well read. He is quite unlike the sour, pinched-nose, sallow-faced naturopaths who lecture everybody with a *jal naiti lota* in one hand and the enema pan hanging from the neck, supported by the rubber pipe over the ears instead of the *janaiu* or sacred thread. I was quite impressed by him and decided to follow his treatment.

Ishwar revolutionized my diet and taught me how to eat sensibly; the various things that can be eaten together and those that should not. What to avoid and what to take for different ailments. The first thing I learnt was that eating dal and curd together is the worst thing possible. This is what we sometimes do in India as we grow older and try unsuccessfully to watch our weight. Those of us who are following a homespun diet will often have a big bowl of dal, a big bowl of curd without rice or chapatti, and feel good about it. We wait expectantly for all our excess fat to melt but it never does. This, I was told, is the worst thing to do as the combination is difficult to digest for it requires different enzymes to induce proper digestion. I then realized that the kosher concept of not mixing proteins and milk products is a healthy one. The Jains are a community which follows such dietary rules, similar to Jewish prohibitions. Jains do not mix dal with milk products. They drink boiled water, but never keep the water for more than eight hours, as it then begins to grow microbes. There are prohibitions on eating leftover food just as there are about eating food that is not in season. These traditional dietary prohibitions are clearly based on a knowledge of the working of the digestive system and the living conditions in specific environments where such dietary laws are required for the health of communities. These are not just rigid taboos based on some fanatical beliefs. It is only the combining of such dietary rules with religious observation that makes them appear unreasonable.

What converted me totally to Ishwar's dietary regulations was my allopathic doctor's discovery during my annual check-up that my kidney was secreting creatinine. The only way I could be treated was to be put on a drip to flush out my whole system. The thought of it was enough to send me into depression. I decided to consult Ishwar who put me on a diet of green vegetables of the pumpkin, zucchini and wax gourd family, which I had for lunch and dinner along with wholewheat chapattis. Much to my doctor's surprise, within fifteen days I was back to normal. He said he would examine me again after I got back to my normal diet. Even after that I was still in the clear and have remained so for the last seven years!

Every time Ishwar would put me on a diet I would experiment with food and come up with delicious recipes. I turned out tasty soups of bottle gourd, *kaddu*, *louki* and *touri*, that people generally find inedible; to eat the wretched things boiled would indeed try the patience of a saint. Ishwar tasted all my concoctions and found them delicious, and wanted me to write a cookbook which he could recommend to his patients. He admitted to me: I put my patients on diets which even I could not stomach for too long, but if they were given your recipes, it would become much easier for them to follow my diet.

This recipe book is thus not a conventional Indian cookbook or a mishmash of different cuisines, but hopefully a more inviting and sensible way to healthy eating. It is also a quick and painless way of cooking for those who enjoy cooking, eating and feeding others without spending hours in the kitchen. I am a firm believer in taking short cuts to cooking and hate the idea of standing over a stove for hours. Nor is my following of healthy food habits a fetish. If frozen vegetables give me enough vitamins and minerals, I shall opt for them any day. I have no desire to compete with members of cordon-bleu clubs by stuffing pasta with toothpicks to get the right aroma. Nor do I need to relax by chopping onions and shedding copious tears and slowly stirring the pot of 110 Indian spices which have been individually roasted and hand pounded. Ouf! The thought of it makes me nervous!

It is possible to make quick, delicious meals with a little improvisation from whatever is available. In fact, improvisation makes for the best cooks, for ingredients are never standardized. Vegetables have a taste, a flavour, depending on the soil conditions, climate and care put into them. Cucumbers can be bitter, but so can aubergines and zucchini. Beans can be tough and stringy and so can asparagus. Thus, no recipe can be absolutely precise. Cooking requires the use of all the senses. Most important, the food should look, smell and taste good. The recipe might call for two cups of water, but your ingredients may require more, or less.

I have always improvised and have never taken any recipe as sacrosanct. I even cheated on my daughter-in-law, who admonished me: Now, Jasleen, no frozen spinach or tomato purée and only free range eggs, please. I quietly went and bought frozen spinach, frozen peas, ready prepared roasted chicken, dried flakes of onion and garlic and grated ginger. Within 15 minutes, I prepared *paalak dahi*, her favourite, and rice with peas. I chopped up the chicken and made a curry with a judicious use of the spices and tomato purée. I dumped the packages in the neighbour's dustbin, and sat down to finish *A Suitable Boy* in peace and quietude. When Australia offered me all the luxuries, except a live-in cook—that too perhaps I could have found, if I had been younger and not merely a visitor to the place— I didn't see why I should not utilize them, just because it was not politically correct.

However, there are certain things I will not use or if I do, only with great caution. I do not like to use white flour or refined sugar, as they are not good for our well-being. I avoid thickening soups in the conventional manner by frying onions and white flour. My soups are either clear or they are a thick purée of vegetables. I do not have recipes for highly-spiced, over-fried food, for I do not think we need to make them. One can indulge once in a while and have *dal makhani*, with naan dripping with ghee, or the delicious *moghlai parantha*, crisp and sinful, and finish off with *gaajar ka halwa* with chunks of *malai*. But I wouldn't encourage anyone to make such food for it is time-consuming and the food is quite indigestible—and I for one, do not know how to make it. So do not look for the typical Indian vegetarian cookbook. If you want to make a Parsi *dhansak*, take the recipe from *The Essential Parsi*

Cookbook by Mrs Manekshaw—the recipe is excellent and the same is the case with *rabri, ras malai, biryani* and stuffed *kachori*.

The main objective of this book is to provide vegetarian recipes which can be effectively used if one is following a diet for correcting the imbalances in the body. It can also form a part of the daily diet as it is tasty and will be able to cater to different tastes, lifestyles and generations. It does not use too much oil, avoids frying and excessive spices. The range of recipes is quite eclectic, from exotic soups with orange juice and carrots to simple *khatte wala saag*, a hot soup with buttermilk, *chulie* and cornflour, to a soup of dried fruits. From the simple *payasam* to an apricot mousse to *aam papad* mousse, I have developed a range of recipes inspired by different cuisines.

My first real introduction to a different kind of cuisine was when I lived in Iran for seven years. My area of specialization being crafts and cottage industries, I had the good fortune of travelling all over Iran and was invited to the homes of people from different parts of the country. I tasted the delicate, sophisticated cuisine of Shiraz, the pink jelly made from wood apple (*beh*), flavoured with cardamom; the green spinach with eggs, called narcissus in the meadow, and *ishkane narenj*, the orange soup. The cuisine of the southern port town of Bandar Abbas was highly spicy in which *shambalele*, fenugreek leaves with tamarind and red chillies, were used as flavouring. There was the delicate cuisine of *shomal*, the Caspian area, *murabba bahar narange*, jam made from fragrant orange flowers, *bagali kotak*, a beans and herb dish, and of course, the extraordinary cuisine of Azerbaijan, which had totally different flavours and richness.

I have given a little background to each vegetable and the range of soups and salads, both raw and cooked. Vegetables are cooked in a variety of ways, and some of these recipes originally used meat. The Persian way of cooking is a subtle combination of vegetables, fruits, herbs and lamb, a symphony of harmonized aromas, flavours and tastes. I have taken a great deal from the Persian cuisine by cooking the vegetables without the meat, but with dry fruit and herbs. When you add a touch of the Indian spices they can become heavenly. *Khoresthe kadu* à la Jasleen is one such dish, the golden coloured peeled pumpkin sautéed with *panch phoron*, a touch of brown sugar and *amchur*—dried mango powder—with dried sour plums and green spinach leaves, is as much a feast for the eyes as for the palate.

I have also absorbed the various influences—the Turkish, the middle eastern as well as African—in my recipes. Included in the book are our own delicacies from Kerala and Bengal, according to me two of the finest cuisines in every sense, and some of my childhood favourites, *kadhi* with vegetables, *mitha chawal* or sweet rice, and *khatte wala saag* made with greens, curd and cornflour.

I have improvised pulao from burgul wheat for those who are allergic to rice and a range of dishes for those with wheat allergies.

This book is meant to initiate people into not just healthy and joyful eating, but also to the joy of cooking, of improvising, of turning out an exciting meal in less than an hour.

So, welcome to Jasleen's Rasoi.

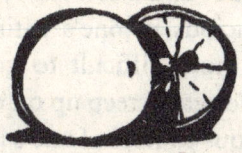

Living with Yourself

Whenever and wherever people get together, discussions on diets inevitably come up. Someone in the family is invariably on a diet: for obesity, anorexia, high cholesterol or for innumerable other reasons. If not their own diets, they express opinions on how others should diet. When my friends corner me and fire me for all my indulgences, I turn around and tell them: My dears, now with HIV, one has to derive one's pleasure from other indulgences. That generally manages to silence them. Whenever I hear of someone who never smoked, never drank, lived life judiciously, and kicked the bucket a bit early, I always tell my friends: Poor guy must have died of deprivation or committed suicide out of boredom.

My son and I have never understood how one cannot be excited about food, and have always found such people quite lacking in humour and a zest for life. Of course, it is necessary to be judicious in one's eating habits and it becomes more and more difficult to go on eating and drinking binges as the years creep up on one. What I have found is that a judicious control of one's intake and a little indulgence now and then, is the best way to organize our dietary life.

We in India are given so many different signals that it is difficult to decide what is really prudent. There is a tendency in the older generation to see the past in a very rosy light, despite having had dismal childhoods and a traumatic youth themselves. The other favourite occupation is to bemoan the lack of sensitivity of the youth and their alienation from traditional culture. My own experience has been quite the opposite. I find the younger generation far better informed than we were at their age and far more aware of the need for a judicious lifestyle.

Despite exposure to Western culture, education and medicine, they are far more aware of the holistic approach to life. There is a greater awareness of ecological balance and also an intense awareness of the overall environment, the outer as well as the inner. They see a link between the diurnal rhythms and the inner rhythms and the close link of the body with the psyche. They may not be aware that the Ayurvedic system is based on these close linkages and cross currents between the state of the body, the mind and the very inner core which works towards a state of perfection and thus to the complete being.

The Indian system recognizes the three constituents of

the being: *Adhibhautic*, the physical being, *Adhidaivic*, the intellectual aspect, and *Adhyatmic*, the divine or the spiritual, as being closely intermingled. *Ayurveda* was derived from the two words, *ayu*—life and *veda*—knowledge, and is thus not merely based on a study of the body, but on life as a whole. The system itself is known as *tridosha*, comprising the three important elements of *vata*, *pita*, *kapha*, which broadly translated mean air or wind, heat or bile, water or phlegm. These three elements when in equilibrium, *doshasamaya*, are in control of the balanced functioning of the body. As we can see, these elements are closely linked with the solar system, the wind, sun, moon, earth and space. They, in turn, are linked with the three *gunas* or qualities—*sattvic*, *rajasik* and *tamasic*. Thus, the body has a direct link with the environment in which it functions, as well as with the mental state of the individual. The sun keeps all creations dry, the moon moistens, while the wind blends the different elements. They nurture the cosmos at the macro level and also at the micro level of the very cells which make up the human body. In the same way, the *tridosha* nurture the physical or the organic state of the body, while the *gunas* are reflected in not only the mental state of being, but in all aspects of life. Human nature is seen as *sattvic*, soothing, calm, with introspective intelligence and is linked with *pita*; *rajasic*, vibrant, vital, outgoing and passionate, is linked with *vata*, while *tamasic* is seen as explosive, uncontrollable, dark and obsessive and is linked with *kapha*. The types of food that the body is fed are seen as being linked not only to the *doshas*, but also with the *gunas* and thus influence the well-being of a person, his/her behaviour and temperament.

This belief in the impact of food was so much a part of our lives that young girls were not allowed to eat spices and proteins as it was felt that these aroused sexual passions. I remember my lovely young cousin, a childhood friend, was not allowed to eat eggs, meat or spices as they were considered 'heating' and by eating them, she would mature too rapidly. In other words, steps were taken to prevent her *rajasic* characteristics from being aroused. She was not allowed to wear bright colours, for even they were *rajasic*, so she always wore pale blue, yellow and cream. The days of such strict regimentation are gone. We are now free to choose our way of life, but freedom of choice requires knowledge and it is the latter which is often lacking. Unfortunately, all those elements of knowledge which are linked to the Indian system are so clouded by their association with religious practices that there is a tendency to be dismissive of them. There is a very simple leitmotif which runs through all Ayurvedic practice: 'If you eat judiciously, you do not need any medicine and if you do not eat judiciously, you do not need any medicine.' A rather simple way to say that no medicine in the world will help if you do not partake of the food suitable to your needs.

The allopathic system that we were treated with, of course, never really looked at food intake the way the Ayurvedic tradition did. In Ayurvedic treatment dietary regulations are as important as the medicine.

My maternal grandmother who had a very strange name, Toti, meaning female parrot, came from a family of Vaids. She was able to diagnose ailments by reading the pulse and was also familiar with the medicinal properties of wild plants which she gathered to prepare concoctions for us. She came to stay with us in Old Delhi after the

Partition and found in me a companion for her rambles as she collected leaves, roots and fruits. Even today I can recognize some of them. She used to say: These doctors give you poison for destroying not just the disease, but also your body and then they aggravate the condition by not telling you what you should eat and what you should not eat, to combat the disease. For her, the thermometer was *bharmameter*—*bharma* being the equivalent of hypochondria.

Naniji was a superb cook and would always tell us to eat food which was full of *rasa*. The word *rasa* has a range of meanings, such as taste, juice, and temperament. In fact, it is the very essence of being. Our theory of aesthetics is based on it, our theory of drama is based on it, and so is the art of cooking. According to the theory of intake of food and healthy eating, there are six *rasas* unlike the *nava rasa*—the nine essences in the theory of aesthetics and drama. The six *rasas* are: sweet, sour, salty, bitter, pungent and astringent and the best meal is that which has a judicious blend of all these. The only cuisines I know which follow these precepts are the Bengali, the Manipuri and the Thai.

Just as important as taste is the need to fulfil all the senses. The sense of smell is of great importance for it gives the first signal to the digestive system as to what is being offered, and for the appropriate digestive juices to be in readiness. Then comes the visual experience when the appearance of the food attracts, followed by the sense of taste and texture. According to the Indian tradition, the sense of smell is the act of *bhog* or partaking.

I also experienced indirectly, through friends, that the

imagination can be a great arouser of appetites. A famous theatre personality of Kerala, Ammannur Madhava Chakkiar, who is a very well-known exponent of Kutiyattam, an extraordinary tradition of classical theatre and story telling, recounted for four hours the preparation of a feast and then the feast itself. By the end of the performance, the audience was so satiated that they did not eat the next day, while others had to take digestives!

Unfortunately, one requires more than just imagination for a balanced diet, which in itself is quite complex. According to Ishwar Sharma, there are some foodstuffs that are good for a person and some that are not. There are various kinds of food that should be eaten together and a few that would cause problems if combined. For instance, one can combine meat and curd (which I personally do not accept) while milk products should not be combined with fish. Black gram (urad dal) should not be eaten with potatoes for it causes acidity and *vayu*. Radish should never be eaten at night as it is *sarad* or cold, causes flatulence, and is hard to digest. But its juice is ideal for curing jaundice. I remember my sister not being allowed to eat a range of things when she was nursing, for it would cause colic to the baby.

Even in allopathy, during my childhood, the doctor used to prescribe a diet for us. I do not know whether the doctor was influenced by his own Indian background or whether that was the practice forty years ago. In my experiences with doctors trained in Europe while I was in Iran, Africa, Switzerland and France, diet played no role, unless it was during the treatment of arteriosclerosis and allergies.

In the past couple of decades, there has been a growing

awareness about healthier eating in the West. The USA, which earlier measured poverty levels by the amount of proteins eaten by a population, has been the most active in educating people to reduce their intake of red meat and encouraging them to eat more vegetables and fibres. In fact, since 1970 the number of heart patients in the USA has gone down significantly, so much so that a number of hospitals closed down their operation theatres which specialized in heart surgery. A carnivorous society is moving towards vegetarianism and has acquired a fascination for Indian and Japanese cuisines.

I think India has probably the richest range of vegetables, both indigenous vegetables, legumes, pulses and lentils and those that have come from the rest of the world. According to scholars researching the food habits of the world, India is supposed to have had an abundance of foodstuff, which provided a rich vegetarian, nutritious diet even as far back as the Harappan times. However, vegetarianism was never a comprehensive practice, though it may have been adhered to by ancient civilizations as they did not wish to deplete their animal stock. Ancient literature talks about the various ways of cooking meat. The prohibition on meat eating began with the common man and not with the Brahmin, for the latter sacrificed animals and thus partook of the feasting that followed such rituals. It is only with the advent of Buddhism and Jainism that vegetarianism became widespread. According to recent census reports, only 25 to 30 per cent of the Indian population is vegetarian, the highest proportion being in Gujarat with 69 per cent, Rajasthan 60, Punjab 54, Haryana and Uttar Pradesh 50 per cent. Kerala, Orissa and West Bengal have the lowest: 6 per cent. However, there are regional variations, for instance, in Bengal people may not eat eggs, but eat fish because it is seen as a fruit of the water. Though the incidence of vegetarianism in India may not be high, yet the normal, everyday food of people is vegetarian owing to economic constraints, except in the coastal belt where fish is plentiful and inexpensive.

The Jains and the Buddhists, being part of the Aryan *shramanic* cults based on earning merit through deed, promoted vegetarianism rather than the Vedic Brahminical tradition of birth, caste and hereditary occupation. In Buddhism and Jainism the basic tenet was ahimsa—non-violence—to all forms of life which extended from the plant to the animal kingdom.

The Bishnoi community located in the Rajasthan desert followed the Jain, Buddhist or Brahminical tradition and the Bishnois are true followers of *ahimsa*. Their twenty-nine rules are based on conservation and the maintenance of ecological balance. I have visited them and found them living in idyllic conditions. A virtual oasis in the middle of the desert is their habitation where birds and animals roam the village without so much as a hint of fear. A fawn was gambolling in the village square as we sat and talked with the village headman. The Bishnoi sect, though only a hundred and fifty years old, has prevented the felling of trees, destroying of shrubs and tubers as well as poaching. They recently apprehended some Bollywood actors who were out poaching in Rajasthan.

Vegetarianism became a way of life for many Indians because of their religious beliefs as well as the need to follow a healthy diet suitable for the geo-climatic conditions. The Jewish and Muslim food prohibitions were essentially connected with the prevention of disease. Certain foods were *mumnoo*—forbidden—and others were *makroo*, permissible, if nothing else was available. Pork was *mumnoo* since the animal lived on waste; so were dead animals and offal. Shell fish were *makroo* as they could easily putrefy and cause food poisoning.

In the West the awareness of food intake being responsible for the state of health has only been researched in the last hundred years. A well-known example is the work done by Dr William Howard Hay at the beginning of this century. He promoted the importance of a proper diet which would nurture the human body and prevent it from becoming toxic and developing chemical imbalance. Unfortunately, his work has been recognized only recently and has not found a place in the curriculum of medical schools. In fact, he came under attack from his own colleagues and was often called a quack.

It was only in the mid-1950s that research on human ecology produced the connection between refined carbohydrates and chemically adulterated food as well as a range of diseases. It still took two decades for the questioning of the theory that all diseases are caused by germs and the acceptance of the fact that diseases could also be caused by genetic, metabolic, behavioural and nutritional deficiencies and imbalances. Today, when we are in the third millennium, the medical profession closely linked with pharmaceutical industries has come to realize the importance of alternative and traditional medicine. This has led to a recognition of other schools of medicine by governments of the more advanced countries. International organizations and medical insurance systems are increasingly recognizing treatment provided under alternative systems. The new approaches to healthy eating habits, exercise, freedom from stress and the need for one's inner self-development are being advocated the world over.

Many of the new approaches to healthy food habits coming to us from the West are, however, not suitable for our dietary habits, traditions, geo-climatic conditions and economic situation. I, for one, firmly believe that if children are encouraged from early childhood to follow a sensible diet and are not force fed, they will automatically opt for the food their system needs.

I had a child rather late in life, and by that time I had suffered the food tantrums of other people's children. I had seen mothers, grandmothers and ayahs pursuing the hapless child up and down the house, heard the stories of diving birds and planes with a piece of food at the end of their beaks or propellers. I was determined never to do that to my child, nor feed him those awful baby foods and the mishmash of insipid food that children are supposed to be weaned with. I used to prepare a thali for my son and put in little bowls of spinach, grated carrots—for everyone in his father's family had weak eyesight—little chapattis and some dal. All the items were cooked the way we ate them, only lightly spiced. I would place the food in front of him and he would sit with us and we would laugh and talk together, and help him, if he wanted or needed help. If he didn't want to eat something, he was not compelled to eat it, but he had to taste it and then decide. There were no tantrums or rude behaviour at table. We addressed the cook with the honorific ji, treated him with respect, thanked him for everything and the child behaved accordingly. It was amazing that the first thing he would finish was his bowl of spinach, then his carrots, and later the other items. Even today, as a young man, his food habits and table manners are better than mine. He never heaps up his plate, he eats things one by one, enjoying each morsel. He avoids using a meal as an occasion for debate, but loves a good discussion at any other time.

The Joy of
Vegetarian
Cooking

Vegetables

a s p a r a g u s

Asparagus is a relatively new delicacy which has only recently become available in our markets, and is sold only in special fruit and vegetable shops. In the West, a wide variety is grown, the most popular and expensive being the white asparagus which is grown underground or covered so that the sun does not get to it. The most delicious is the wild asparagus, grown now in a number of vegetable gardens in India in the suburbs of the large cities. Asparagus is, however, an ancient vegetable known to have been cultivated by the Egyptians. The Roman epicures prized it highly for its flavour and may also have considered it an aphrodisiac, a belief that the English inherited from them.

ASPARAGUS SOUP

Serves 4

Salt and pepper to taste
1 bunch fresh young green asparagus, approx. 250 gm
3 cloves garlic, crushed
2 tsp cornflour
1 tsp lime juice

In a wide pan pour 3 cups water, salt and pepper. Lay the asparagus flat in the pan. Boil for 5 minutes.

Drain, reserving liquid.

With a sharp knife, cut off 2" of the top of asparagus and gently remove to one side.

Put the liquid back in pan and add crushed garlic and bottom ends of asparagus. In ½ cup cold water mix cornflour and add to pan. Boil for 10 minutes or until tender.

Run through liquidizer and then sieve and remove any strings.

Add lime juice and salt to taste.

Serve hot or cold, adding 3 spears of asparagus to each bowl of soup.

Serve remaining asparagus spear heads as a side dish with vinaigrette sauce.

ASPARAGUS SANDWICHES ROLLED

8 small spears asparagus
Salt to taste
Mustard to taste
Pepper to taste
3 tbsp butter
4 thin slices brown bread

- Boil the spears of asparagus and set aside or use the leftovers from previous recipe.

- Mix salt, mustard and pepper with butter.

- Cut the crust from bread and halve.

- Roll the bread slice with a rolling pin.

- Butter the slices.

- Place the asparagus on one side and roll. Hold together with a toothpick, trimming it.

- Toast in oven at 180°C before serving.

ASPARAGUS SALAD WITH EGGS

Serves 4

1 small head lettuce
1 bunch cooked asparagus, chopped
3 hard-boiled eggs, chopped
6 stuffed olives, cut in roundels
1 tbsp capers
¼ cup mayonnaise
¼ cup vinaigrette sauce
½ tsp chilli sauce

- Line a bowl with washed and dried, crisp large lettuce leaves. Break the remainder into pieces.

- Mix asparagus, eggs, smaller lettuce leaves, olives and capers.

- Mix mayonnaise and the two sauces and pour onto the mixture. Toss lightly.

- Pour into the lined salad bowl and serve immediately.

aubergine

There is a funny story regarding aubergine, based on the folk version of the tales of Akbar and Birbal that Mohammed Yunus, Indira Gandhi's roving ambassador, recounted to the Shah at a formal dinner in Iran in the early seventies. The main protagonist was the aubergine: A Padshah was served an aubergine and the cook praised his dish saying, Oh master, see this magnificent aubergine dressed in purple robes of royalty, with a green emerald crown on its head, made now into a delectable dish for the ruler of the world. As he spoke, the master tasted the dish, decided he did not like aubergine, and pushed it aside.

The cook took his cue and changed his tune, saying: How right you are! I have been blinded. It is a miserable bandicoot, see how ugly is its shape and its wretched tail. He picked it up by its curling stem and threw it out of the window. The Padshah remarked: Well! A minute ago you were praising it to the skies, now what has happened? To which the cook quipped: Your Royal Majesty, it is not the aubergine who employs me.

The story made the Shah laugh uproariously. Suddenly the atmosphere, which had so far been formal and cool, became relaxed and the negotiations proceeded smoothly. I was told this story by Ram Sathe who was then India's ambassador to Iran.

The Indian name for aubergine is baingan, which people who do not like the vegetable interpret as *bey gun*—without merit. It is actually derived from the Sanskrit *vatinganah*, which translates as that which causes no wind. In Gujarati they use the word *vatana*. This points to the fact that the aubergine's origins are Asian, possibly Indian. The aubergine is a great favourite in the Middle East and is an important constituent of the Middle Eastern cuisine. Iranians love aubergine, and cook it peeled, which has given rise to a number of jokes about them. One which is common is that if a woman peels more than five long aubergines, she has to have a purificatory bath.

The aubergine has a distinct flavour and texture which lends itself to a range of dishes. I cook either with mustard oil or with butter. So when I refer to oil, I mean mustard oil. If any other oil is meant, it is spelt out. Mustard oil is healthy and pungent. It needs to be heated to be rid of its strong smell. If you don't like mustard oil, then use butter, corn or sunflower oil.

POOR MAN'S CAVIAR

Serves 6

1 large head lettuce
2 bunches mint
100 gm green coriander
4 spring onions
½ cup malt vinegar
¼ cup soya sauce
2 tsp chilli sauce
Oil as required
3 round aubergines, approx. 1 kg
1 large onion, finely chopped
2 tbsp lime juice
4 walnuts, crushed
Salt to taste

In a flat tray or large platter, arrange washed and dried lettuce leaves, sprigs of mint and half the green coriander, onion heads cut into thin, long pieces and the green stems sliced into 2" pieces.

· Mix vinegar and soya sauce in a bowl.

· Put chilli sauce in a small bowl.

· Rub a little oil on the aubergines and roast on the flame until the skins are burnt black. Alternatively, cut into half, rub oil on the cut section and put into an oven or microwave. In the oven, at a temperature of 200° C, it should cook through in 15 to 20 minutes. In a microwave, it should take 8 minutes. Direct roasting is ideal for it gives a smoky aroma.

· After it's been roasted on the flame, cool and peel all

the skin away, for that burnt flavour. If cooked in an oven or microwave, scoop out the flesh and discard skin.

· Mash aubergines, removing pockets of seed, if any.

· Chop the remaining coriander and mix with aubergines, onion, lime juice, walnut and salt. Taste for salt and lemony flavour and put in a bowl. Place bowl in the tray prepared with the greens and serve.

· This is to be eaten before a meal. Take a leaf of salad, put a tablespoon of aubergine, some mint, coriander and spring onions on it. Sprinkle vinegar and soya sauce and add a touch of chilli. Roll the salad leaf and enjoy.

This is fun food which is also non-fattening, so even those on a diet can enjoy it. Keep a supply of salad leaves ready, washed and dried, in case more are needed.

A middle eastern salad, Baba Ganoush, is made in a similar way as the aubergine mix used here. Only, add a paste made of 100 gm roasted sesame seeds, with ¼ teaspoon cumin powder and additional lime juice.

BAINGAN BHARTHA

Aubergine Puréed

Serves 6

3 large round aubergines, approx. 1 kg
1 large onion
6 cloves garlic
2 tbsp mustard oil or ghee
1 pinch asafoetida powder
2 dry red chillies
Salt to taste
2 tbsp lime juice
2 tbsp chopped green coriander

· Roast aubergines as described in the recipe for Poor Man's Caviar (p. 11-12).

· If roasted on an open flame, after removing the charred skin, put into a colander and wash well. Keep in colander for the liquid to drip out.

· After 20 minutes, put the roasted aubergines in a wide bowl, hold the stem with the left hand and with a fork mash the flesh separating it from the top of the aubergines. Retain stem and take care not to denude it of all flesh. Mash the aubergines well and set aside.

· Chop onion coarsely and slice garlic very fine.

· In a kadhai heat oil until it smokes. Remove from fire and add a pinch of asafoetida, whole red chillies, and return to the fire. Fry for half a minute.

· Add chopped onions and garlic and stir-fry until

onions are transparent.

- Add aubergines and tops of aubergines. Sprinkle salt. Stir-fry on a high flame for five minutes.

- Add lime juice and half the green coriander.

- Cook for another 2 minutes.

- Serve hot with the remaining coriander sprinkled on top.

BAINGAN BHARTHA RAITA

Puréed Aubergine with Curd

Serves 6

2 aubergines, approx. 500 gm
1 small onion, finely chopped
1½ tbsp chopped green coriander
2 cups curd, beaten smooth
1 level tsp salt
½ tsp black pepper
¼ tsp red chilli powder
2 tbsp coarsely chopped walnuts

- Prepare aubergines as for Poor Man's Caviar (p. 11-12).

- Mix onion, 1 tbsp coriander and all the other ingredients, except curd.

- Mix well using a fork.

- Add curd and mix.

- Transfer to a serving dish and garnish with remaining green coriander.

- Refrigerate before serving.

ROYAL SLIPPERS

Stuffed Aubergine

Serves 6

3 large aubergines, approx. 1 kg
2 tbsp butter
2 small onions, finely chopped
6 cloves garlic, finely chopped
2 tomatoes
4 tbsp chopped walnuts
2 tbsp chopped green mint
¼ tsp chilli powder
½ tsp pepper
1 level tsp salt
Juice of 1 lime

- Cut aubergines lengthwise and place on a tray with the cut side buttered.

- Bake in an oven at 250° C for 10 minutes until the insides of aubergines are cooked. Remove from oven.

- With a spoon scoop out flesh, taking care to leave some adhering to the sides so that the aubergines are firm.

- Fry onion and garlic in 1 tablespoon butter until transparent.

- Add mashed aubergine, cook for 3 minutes.

- While the aubergines are cooking, put tomatoes in boiling liquid for 1 minute. Remove from water and skin. Chop fine and add to the cooking aubergines. Mix well.

- Cook for 5 minutes or until the liquid of tomatoes is absorbed, leaving mixture moist.

- Remove from fire, add chopped walnuts, ½ tablespoon mint, chilli powder, pepper, salt, lime juice and 1 tbsp butter.

- Fill aubergine shells with the mixture. Spread butter on top and sprinkle green mint.

- Bake in oven in a buttered dish at 250° C for 10 minutes.

- Serve hot.

REMBRANDT'S DISH

Aubergine with Mixed Vegetables

Serves 6

3 large round aubergines, approx. 750 gm
4 zucchini, approx. 500 gm
3 capsicums, approx. 500 gm
500 gm yellow pumpkin
4 onions
10 cloves garlic
4 tbsp olive oil
½ tsp black peppercorns
1 tsp cumin seeds
1 tsp coriander seeds
¼ tsp fenugreek seeds
3 dry red chillies
20 fresh basil leaves
4 bay leaves
500 gm tomatoes, skinned and chopped
1 heaped tbsp brown sugar
Golf ball-size lump of tamarind, soaked and juiced
Salt to taste
A few fresh basil leaves

· Cut aubergines into ½" thick roundels. Cut in triangles so that one side of each piece has the purple skin. Salt pieces and put in a colander to drain out liquid.

· Cut zucchini in ½" thick roundels, add salt and put to drain in separate colander.

· Cut capsicum in roundels, discard seeds.

- Skin yellow pumpkin and cut into bite-size pieces.
- Cut onions in ¼" thick roundels.
- Chop garlic.
- In a large pan add olive oil and all the spices. When the seeds begin to pop, add onion and garlic. Stir-fry until transparent.
- Add aubergines and sauté for 5 minutes until they are brown. Lower flame, cover and cook for 8 minutes.
- Increase flame slightly, add capsicum, stir gently together. Cook covered for 2 minutes.
- Add zucchini and stir together. Take care to keep the pieces whole. Cook for 5 minutes covered.
- Finally add pumpkin pieces, stirring them in with care. Cook covered for 3 minutes.
- Add chopped tomatoes, brown sugar, tamarind juice and salt and cook for 5 minutes.
- Check the aubergines; they should be done by now.
- Remove lid and cook for 5 minutes or till the juices evaporate.
- Add fresh basil leaves and mix together.
- Serve hot.

This dish takes a little time to cook, but it is delicious and has the most wonderfully rich appearance like a still life of Rembrandt. It also retains the individual colours, although subdued. The purple becomes less brazen, the yellow becomes ochre and the green of zucchini looks like old jade, while the thick roundels of green capsicum shine with twin shades of green. The fresh basil adds colour and flavour and the spices their aroma and rich taste.

It is important to stir gently. My mother used to stir such dishes with a spatula and in the last stages used the long flat handle to stir gently. Perhaps instead of a pan you could use a wok for cooking.

You will find people mopping up the sauce with bread or with naan which should be served on the side.

AUBERGINE SANDWICH

Snacks for a small party

Serves 6

3 large aubergines, approx. 1 kg
Salt to taste
1 cup home-made cottage cheese (paneer)
1 onion, finely chopped
1 tsp pomegranate seeds (anardana), finely pounded
½ tsp chilli powder
3 tbsp chopped mint
6 tbsp oil
2 eggs, beaten
½ cup breadcrumbs

- Cut aubergines in ¼" thick roundels. Cut further into three or four triangular pieces. Sprinkle salt, put on a round tray at an angle and drain water.

- Mix paneer, onion, pomegranate seeds, salt, chilli powder and mint.

- Heat a griddle, rub a little oil on aubergine pieces and fry until brown on both sides.

- Spread paneer mixture on one piece and place another piece on top, pressing down firmly.

- Spread a little salt in the egg. Spread breadcrumbs in a plate. Dip aubergine sandwich in egg and then coat with breadcrumbs.

- In a griddle heat 2 tsp oil and shallow fry the sandwich on both sides until brown. Drain on absorbent paper. Repeat the process with the other aubergine pieces. Serve hot.

21

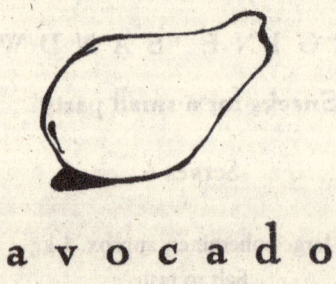

avocado

Avocado comes from the Aztec word Ahucati, meaning testicle tree, possibly because of the large seed inside. There is an interesting story of how it gained popularity. A group of avocado producers published a denial of the rumours that avocados were an aphrodisiac, as a result of which the sales shot up immediately! We are told that there are 700 varieties of avocados. I am familiar with only the pear-shaped avocado, which is easy to peel and has a creamy texture. There is another variety which turns from dark green to purple when ripe.

My introduction to avocados was via my friend Sunand who used to get the smelly breadfruit from Bangalore. So little were avocados thought of that they were used as stuffing when breadfruits were packed. Avocados grew in plenty in Sunand's garden and were not greatly valued. We would sprinkle salt, pepper and lime juice and enjoy it as a glorious snack.

When avocados began arriving in Delhi at stores which sold fruit to foreigners, I learnt of other ways to eat them, until I became addicted.

Recently, in Australia, I visited a young couple in the Wollongong area. They had this wonderful avocado tree which bore fruit all the year round. The avocados ripened only after they were plucked. My hosts served avocado sandwiches, avocado salad and avocado mousse and I was in heaven.

AVOCADO DELIGHT

Serves 4

2 ripe avocados
6 tbsp French dressing

- Cut avocados lengthwise.
- Remove seeds. Put in its place the dressing and serve as a starter.

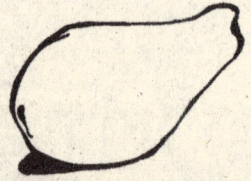

GUACAMOLE

Serves 4

2 ripe avocados, peeled and chopped
2 tbsp chopped green coriander
1 green chilli, finely chopped
Juice of 2 limes
1 onion, finely chopped
Salt to taste

· Mix all ingredients and run through a liquidizer. Transfer to a bowl.

· Serve with crisp toast or crisped quarters of leftover chapatti.

AVOCADO MOUSSE

Serves 4

2 ripe avocados
1 tsp wine vinegar
Juice of 1 lime
½ tsp salt
Dash of tabasco
¾ tsp gelatin
1 tbsp chopped parsley or green coriander
4 almonds, blanched and pounded coarsely

- Cut each avocado in half, remove seed and carefully scoop out the flesh. Reserve shells of avocado; rub with lime juice to prevent discolouration.

- Purée the flesh with vinegar, lime juice, salt and tabasco.

- Put 2 tbsp cold water into the gelatin and mix. Add 2 tbsp boiling water and mix it all together briskly. Add to the avocado mix and purée once again.

- Add parsley and almonds and mix together.

- Spoon the mixture into the avocado shells and smooth the top.

- Refrigerate for a couple of hours.

AVOCADO SALAD

Serves 4

2 large avocados
1½ tbsp lime juice
2 tomatoes, cut into bite-size pieces
2 sticks celery, finely chopped
1 small onion, finely chopped
4 tbsp French dressing
½ lime, cut into 4 wedges

· Cut avocados lengthwise and remove seeds.

· Remove the flesh carefully with a spoon and chop. Immediately add ½ tbsp lime juice and mix.

· Rub lime juice on the inside of the avocado to prevent discolouration.

· Mix all the ingredients together.

· Heap the salad into the avocado shells, and serve with wedges of lime.

AVOCADO AND GRAPEFRUIT SALAD

Serves 4

2 ripe avocados, peeled and chopped
2 grapefruits, separated, and segments skinned and cut
2 tbsp chopped mint
½ tsp powdered sugar
½ tsp salt
Juice of 1 lime
Dash of tabasco

- Place avocado in a bowl with grapefruit segments.

- Sprinkle chopped mint, sugar, salt, lime juice and tabasco and toss together.

- Serve in a wooden bowl.

b e a n s

Beans are supposed to have come from the Americas, but I am sure they must have grown here as well, for we have such a variety of beans, including *sem ki phalli, papardi, surati papardi*, French beans, red beans, haricot beans, runner beans, broad beans and *lobia* of many varieties. It was in Gujarat that I was taught how versatile beans are. The *sem phalli* would be dried and crisply fried to be eaten with rice or nibbled by the more sophisticated with a glass of beer. The tender young curved beans of *surati papardi* were specially prepared for the delicately flavoured mixed vegetable *oundhia* that was made for 14 January, the festival of Makar Sankranti which welcomed the sun as it began its northerly movement. The wind changed direction, myriads of coloured kites were flown during the day and the air was filled with the sound of fluttering kites and shouts of the kite fliers. The medley of vegetables cooked in a sealed clay pot would be opened in the afternoon and its rich aroma would rise up to the rooftop, bringing the veteran kite fliers down to savour the *oundhia*.

Beans are versatile and can be made into salads, soups, curries and stir-fried dishes. Dried beans, from the small black-eyed beans to the large kidney beans, serve as important protein components for a vegetarian diet, while green beans contain a great deal of vitamins and phosphates. According to the Ayurvedic tradition they need to be eaten with care as they can cause flatulence. In Jane Grigsons' *Vegetable Book*, reference is made to *Dios Corides*, written in the first century AD, which described beans as 'windy, flatulent, hard on digestion, causing troublesome dreams'.

BEANS WITH SESAME SALAD

Serves 6

750 gm young French beans
1 tsp salt
¼ cup sesame seeds
½ tsp black sesame seeds
3 tbsp sesame oil or corn oil
2 tbsp malt vinegar
2 tbsp light soya sauce
½ tbsp chilli sauce

- String beans and break into 2½" pieces. Drop into boiling water. Add ½ tsp salt. Cook for 10 minutes without lid. Check to ensure that beans are cooked but not soft. Drain and set aside.

- In a frying pan roast sesame seeds, stirring for a very short while. Do not brown. Take off the fire. Reserve one-third of the seeds and place the rest in a mortar and pound into a thick paste.

- Mix all the ingredients together and pour over beans. Mix well together.

- Before serving, mix together again. Lift with tongs and arrange lengthwise in a dish. Pour the sauce over it. Sprinkle with whole sesame seeds.

Black sesame seeds are rich in calcium and very healthy. It is better to use these rather than the white ones, which are sesame seeds with the skin removed. However, the black sesame is slightly bitter, so you could mix the two according to your taste.

31

FRENCH BEAN SALAD

Serves 4

250 gm French beans
1 tbsp olive oil
2 tsp lime juice
1 tbsp chopped onions
½ tsp salt
¼ tsp chilli sauce (optional)
1 tbsp peanuts, roasted

- Wash beans and string. Break into half.

- Put in boiling water. Do not cover.

- When the beans are boiled but firm, strain.

- In a bowl, mix all ingredients except peanuts.

- Coarsely grind peanuts and add half to beans. Reserve the other half.

- Arrange the prepared salad in a bowl, sprinkle the remaining peanuts on top and refrigerate before serving.

MIXED VEGETABLE SALAD

Serves 6

1 head lettuce, washed and dried
250 gm boiled French beans
250 gm tomatoes
100 gm sprouted green gram (sabut moong)
1 large onion, cut in roundels
2 sticks celery, chopped
½ cup French dressing

- Mix all vegetables together.
- Pour French dressing over the vegetables, mix well and serve.

STRING BEANS WITH TOMATOES

Serves 6

2 tbsp butter
500 gm beans, strung and cut into 1" pieces
6 cloves garlic, finely chopped
½ tsp black cumin, roasted and powdered
500 gm tomatoes, skinned and chopped
¼ tsp allspice
¼ tsp chilli powder
¼ cup chopped green coriander
2 tbsp lime juice

- Put butter in a wok. Add beans, garlic, cumin and sauté for 2 minutes.

- Add tomatoes on top, sprinkle allspice, chilli powder and coriander. Add ¼ cup hot water from the side, and salt.

- Close lid tightly, lower flame and simmer for 10 to 12 minutes. Check if beans are cooked. If necessary, add a little more water and cook until beans are tender but firm.

- Remove lid and add lime juice. Cook for 2 minutes with the lid open, if too watery.

- This dish can be served hot or cold.

BEAN PORIYAL

Dry Beans

Serves 6

2 tbsp oil
1 dry red chilli
1 pinch asafoetida powder
1 tsp cumin seeds
1 sprig curry leaves
1 tsp mustard seeds
1 tsp black gram (urad dal), washed
1 tsp Bengal gram (chana dal), washed
500 gm French beans, finely chopped
Salt to taste
2 tbsp freshly grated coconut, or 2½ tbsp dried coconut

· Heat oil in thick-bottomed wok. When it smokes add whole red chilli and asafoetida and remove from fire.

· Add all the spices and curry leaves and stir together. When the mustard seeds splutter add the chopped beans, salt and ¼ cup water. Close lid and simmer on low fire for 15 minutes. Stir every few minutes. If necessary, sprinkle more water and close lid until beans are done.

· Add the coconut and mix thoroughly.

HARA LOBIA VA MOONGPHALI SABZI

Green Beans and Peanuts

Serves 6

2 tbsp oil

2 dry red chillies

1 pinch asafoetida powder

500 gm long green beans (hara lobia), finely chopped

4 garlic cloves, finely chopped

½ tsp turmeric powder

½ tsp coriander powder

½ tsp cumin powder

½ tsp dried mango powder (amchur)

½ tsp salt

4 tbsp raw peanuts

- Heat oil in a wok. When it smokes, take off the fire. Add dry chillies and asafoetida.

- Return to fire and add beans, garlic and all the spices. Sprinkle ¼ cup water and salt and cover. Cook for 8 minutes on a low fire.

- Remove lid and stir till all the spices are mixed.

- In a frying pan roast the peanuts slightly brown till the skin begins to come off. Take off the fire, remove skin by rubbing together and blow the skin off.

- Crush the peanuts coarsely, add to beans and mix together. This method can be followed to cook French beans as well.

GREEK STEWED BEANS

Serves 6

3 tbsp olive oil
1 dry red chilli
2 onions, sliced long and thin
4 cloves garlic, crushed
2 bay leaves
750 gm French beans, strung and snapped in half
500 gm tomatoes, skinned and coarsely chopped
Salt and pepper to taste
¼ tsp rosemary, finely chopped
½ tsp cumin powder

· Heat oil in saucepan and put in red chilli.

· Add onion and sauté until transparent. Then add garlic and bay leaves and stir for half a minute.

· Place beans on top and over that the tomatoes. Sprinkle salt, pepper, rosemary and cumin. Add ¼ cup water. Cover and simmer on low fire for 15 to 20 minutes. Keep an eye on the liquid level; if it gets dry, add more water.

· This can be eaten hot with rice or cold as a salad.

MASALA BEANS

Serves 6

2 tbsp oil
1 dry red chilli
1 pinch asafoetida powder
1 tsp black gram (urad dal), washed
1 tsp Bengal gram (chana dal), washed
500 gm fresh beans, strung and chopped
Salt to taste

For paste:

1 tsp oil
1 tsp cumin seeds
2 tsp mustard seeds
3 dry red chillies
½ coconut, grated
2 tbsp malt vinegar
2 tbsp water
1 sprig curry leaves

- Heat oil in thick-bottomed wok.

- Add red chilli, black gram, Bengal gram, asafoetida and fry for half a minute. Add beans and saute for 2 minutes.

- Add salt and ½ cup water. Stir. Close lid and simmer on slow fire for 15 minutes. Stir frequently. Add water, if necessary, and cook until beans are cooked.

Paste:
- Put 1 tsp oil in a frying pan and roast dry spices, red

chillies and grated coconut.

· Cool and put in liquidizer with vinegar, water, curry leaves and make into paste.

· Return cooked beans to fire, heat thoroughly and add prepared paste. If necessary, add ¼ cup water.

· Cover and simmer for 2 minutes.

· Serve with chapatti or rice.

bottle gourd &
other gourds

Bottle gourd or louki is a vegetable the very mention of which as a child would send me into tantrums. My cousin and I would sneak out of our rooms in the summer heat, while everyone else had their siesta, and try to destroy the bottle gourd plants that grew so abundantly in the garden and which therefore formed a part of our summer cuisine. It is only recently when I was put on a bottle gourd diet that I realized how tasty even this vegetable can be. As a soup it is delectable, and made into a pickle it is delicious. What we have to remember is that it is a miracle vegetable which cleanses the system and can set right the toxic imbalances in the body. It is cooling and is prescribed as a diet for those suffering from intermittent fever.

There are a range of vegetables which belong to this family—zucchini, squash, small round light green tindas, wax gourd or *parmal*, ridged gourd or *touri*, snake gourd, and tiny speckled *tindola*, often mistakenly called gherkins. These are an important part of our diet. Also, those suffering from heat stroke get respite if the soles of their feet and the top of the head are rubbed with pieces of bottle gourd, as it extracts heat from the system.

PURÉED DELIGHT SOUP

Bottle Gourd Soup

Serves 6

1 kg bottle gourd, squash or zucchini
6 almonds, soaked, blanched, peeled and cut into thin, long slivers
8 cloves garlic, finely chopped
2 leaves of lemon grass tied in a knot (optional)
½ tsp salt
Juice of 2 limes
1 tbsp chopped mint or basil leaves
¼ tsp chilli sauce (optional)

- Clean bottle gourd thoroughly with water by rubbing the skin. Cut into small pieces with the skin intact.

- Heat 6 cups water in a pan with garlic and lemon grass.

- Add salt to taste.

- When the water boils, add the vegetable. Cook for 15 to 20 minutes or until soft.

- Take off fire and cool.

- Remove lemon grass leaves from the soup and discard.

- Mix in blender, adding juice of 2 limes. The soup should have a lemony tang but should not be too sour. As the size of limes varies, taste after adding juice of one lime.

- Add slivers of almond and chopped mint or basil.

- Serve with toasted bread.
- This soup can be served hot or cold. For those who like a hot chilli taste, add ¼ tsp chilli sauce.

A thing to remember is not to tell your guests the contents of the soup. People invariably ask, 'Now what is this?' and depending on the company and my mood, I give it a number of names: jade delicious, spring delight, hari sugat—green gift or Krishna's gift. We all have childhood antipathies and usually bottle gourd, *kaddu*, squash and carrots top the list.

FRESH YOUNG ZUCCHINI SALAD

Serves 4

500 gm young small-sized zucchini, scraped in alternate strips and
cut in roundels
250 gm tomatoes, cut in roundels
1 large onion, finely chopped
½ cup French dressing

- Mix all vegetables together with the dressing and refrigerate for 1 hour before serving.

For visitors from abroad who are warned not to eat uncooked vegetables, the salad can be made as follows:

- Boil a large pan of water. When the water boils, add the washed zucchini. Let the water come to a boil again, then drain the zucchini and cool.

- Put tomatoes in boiling water and skin.

- Chop zucchini and tomatoes into roundels.

- Mix all the ingredients while the vegetables are hot. Refrigerate and then serve.

TINDA AND MINT SALAD

Serves 4

500 gm tinda, lightly scraped and quartered
1 bunch mint, cleaned and chopped
1 small onion, finely chopped
½ cup French dressing

· Boil tinda for 5 minutes and drain.

· Mix with mint, onion and dressing.

· Refrigerate for 1 hour before serving.

This can also be made with raw tinda by chopping the tinda into very thin roundels and tossing together with all the ingredients.

TINDA MASALEDAR

Serves 6

500 gm tinda (tender ones)
½ tsp coriander powder
½ tsp cumin powder
1 tsp dried mango powder (amchur)
¼ tsp fine chilli powder, not too pungent
½ tsp salt
3 tbsp oil

· Slit the tinda ¼ of the way with a cross cut.

· Mix all the spices together and push the mixture into the slit with your fingers.

· Heat oil in a wok.

· Remove from heat and put in the tindas open-side up.

· Sauté for 5 minutes, stirring.

· Sprinkle water generously. Cover and simmer for 8 minutes or until the tindas are done. Keep sprinkling water to prevent them from burning.

· Serve hot.

TINDOLA SALAD

Serves 4

500 gm tindola
1 onion, finely chopped
½ cup French dressing

- Cut tindola lengthwise into half. Discard those that have many seeds or are red in colour. Boil for 8 minutes and drain.

- Mix with onion and dressing.

- Refrigerate for 1 hour before serving.

LOUKI AUR MILI-JULI SABZIAN

Bottle Gourd, Onion, Capsicum and Aubergine

Serves 6

3 tbsp butter
1 kg bottle gourd, cut in roundels
2 aubergines, cut in roundels
2 capsicums, deseeded and cut in roundels
2 onions, cut in roundels
1 onion, finely chopped
8 cloves garlic, finely chopped
1 tsp cumin powder
½ tsp coriander powder
¼ tsp chilli powder
Salt to taste
½ cup cream
1½ tbsp butter
Pepper to taste
2 bay leaves

· Rub a little butter on a griddle using a cut potato. Place roundels of bottle gourd, aubergine, capsicum and onion on the griddle. Toast individually and set aside.

· Heat 2 tbsp butter in a pan, and sauté the chopped onion and garlic. Add spices and salt. Cook until onions are a golden brown. Remove from fire, add ½ cup cream and mix to make a sauce.

· Take a baking dish and lightly rub butter on all sides. Place a layer of aubergines and sprinkle a pinch of salt and pepper. Pour 2 tbsp of the sauce. Add 1 bay leaf. Put a double layer of bottle gourd followed by 1 layer of onions, add 1 bay leaf and a little sauce. Place the remaining bottle gourd and onion and top the layer with aubergines. Pour the remaining sauce.

Preheat oven to 250° C, bake for 20 to 25 minutes and serve.

LOUKI KA RAITA

Bottle Gourd with Curd

Serves 6

500 gm bottle gourd
2 cups home-made curd
1 onion, finely chopped
¼ tsp chilli powder (optional)
20 raisins, washed and soaked in water
½ tsp salt
1½ tbsp mint, chopped

- Wash and scrape skin of bottle gourd and grate.

- Boil half a pan of water. Add grated bottle gourd and boil for 2 minutes. Remove and drain in colander.

- Whisk curd with a little water.

- Mix boiled bottle gourd with curd, onion and chilli powder.

- Add raisins after discarding water. Garnish with chopped mint.

- Refrigerate.

- Add salt only just before serving or the raita might become watery.

- Serve with chapatti or rice.

49

BOTTLE GOURD KOFTA CURRY

Serves 6

500 gm bottle gourd, grated
1 onion, finely chopped
1" ginger, finely grated
1 cup chickpea flour (besan)
½ tsp salt
¼ tsp chilli powder
¼ tsp bishop's weed (ajwain)
4 tbsp mustard oil

For sauce:

2 onions, finely chopped
6 cloves garlic, finely chopped
1 bay leaf
½ tsp turmeric powder
¼ tsp cumin powder
¼ tsp chilli powder
1 pinch asafoetida
3 tomatoes, skinned and chopped fine
Salt to taste

- Mix the grated bottle gourd with onion and ginger.

- Add salt, chilli powder and ajwain to the besan.

- Add ¼ cup water to the besan and mix to make a thick batter. Add the vegetable mix and stir to ensure that there are no lumps.

- Make small balls (koftas) of the besan-vegetable mixture.

- Heat oil in a kadhai. When the oil smokes, add the koftas with a spoon so as not to splash, and deep fry until brown. Remove koftas with a perforated spoon and place on an absorbent paper towel.

- Remove kadhai from fire and drain oil, retaining 2 tbsp in the kadhai.

Sauce:

- Add onion and garlic and fry until transparent.

- Add all the spices and sauté for 1 minute.

- Add tomatoes and stir briskly for 2 minutes.

- Add 1 cup water and bring to a boil.

- Add koftas to sauce and simmer for ten minutes.
- Serve hot with chapatti, naan or rice.

GHIA ACHAAR
Bottle Gourd Pickle

1 kg bottle gourd
100 gm red mustard powder
1½ tsp salt
½ tsp chilli powder
½ tsp bishop's weed (ajwain)

- Wash bottle gourd and cut into ½" roundels. Cut further into triangular pieces so that each piece has the peel.

- Put bottle gourd in boiling water. Keep for 1 minute and drain immediately. Spread on an absorbent towel and allow the water to drain off and the vegetable to cool.

- Transfer to a bowl and add all the spices, rubbing them well into the pieces with your hands.

- Fill into a bottle, cover mouth with a cloth. Keep in the sun for 2 to 3 days, shaking it every 3 hours.

- The achaar should be ready. Serve with meals as a tasty side dish and also with drinks.

- Keep refrigerated and use within 10 days.

GHIA TAMATAR TARKARI

Bottle Gourd or Zucchini and Tomatoes

Serves 6

2 tbsp mustard oil
2 dry red chillies
1 tsp cumin seeds
1 pinch asafoetida powder
3 large onions, cut in roundels
6 cloves garlic, crushed
1 kg zucchini, scraped in alternate strips and cut in thick roundels. If
using bottle gourd, scrape skin lightly and cut into bite-size pieces
½ tsp turmeric powder
¼ tsp chilli powder (optional)
250 gm tomatoes, cut in thick roundels
Salt to taste

- Put mustard oil in kadhai and heat. When it begins to smoke, add whole dry chillies, cumin and asafoetida.

- Add onion and stir. Add garlic and sauté on low fire till golden in colour.

- Add zucchini and the spices. Sauté for one to three minutes until the turmeric begins to give out its aroma.

- Add tomatoes on top and cover the pan as it begins to simmer.

- Put a metal plate at the bottom of the kadhai, so as to lower the temperature.

- Sprinkle about ¼ cup water and cook for 15 minutes.
- Bottle gourd, squash and snake gourd can all be cooked in the same way. If you are on a diet on account of digestive problems, kidney malfunctioning or respiratory problems, omit tomatoes.

GHIA BHARTHA

Bottle Gourd Puréed

Serves 6

1 kg round bottle gourd
2 tbsp oil
2 dry red chillies
¼ tsp asafoetida powder
2 onions, coarsely chopped
6 cloves garlic, finely chopped
½ tsp salt
Juice of 1 lime
1 bunch green coriander or mint, chopped

· The round variety of bottle gourd makes the best bhartha but young long ones can also be used.

· On an open gas flame burn the rind of bottle gourd. Remove rind under water, cut the bottle gourd and mash.

· Put oil in a kadhai, heat till it smokes, add chillies and asafoetida, fry for half a minute.

· Add onion and garlic, sauté until onions are transparent.

· Add the bottle gourd and sauté for 5 minutes.

· Add ⅓ cup water and salt, cover and cook for five minutes.

· Add lime juice, garnish with coriander or mint, and serve.

GHIA DUDH SABZI

Bottle Gourd with Milk

Serves 6

1 kg bottle gourd
1 tbsp oil
2 dry red chillies
½ tsp cumin seeds
1 onion, coarsely chopped
3 cloves garlic, chopped
1 cup milk
½ tsp salt

- Cut bottle gourd into bite-size pieces after lightly scraping skin.
- Heat oil. Add chillies and cumin and stir for half a minute.
- Add onion and garlic and fry lightly for less than 1 minute. Add vegetable.
- Sauté briskly for 2 minutes on a high flame.
- Sprinkle ¼ cup water. Cover and lower flame. Simmer for 6 to 7 minutes, stirring. Add water, if necessary.
- When the vegetable is nearly done, add milk and stir. Cook for 2 minutes covered, then remove lid and cook for 5 minutes.
- Add salt only after the vegetable is cooked, otherwise the milk will curdle.
- Serve with chapatti or rice.

SNAKE GOURD KOOTU/STEW

Serves 6

½ cup pigeon peas (toor/arhar dal)
500 gm snake gourd, chopped

For paste:

2 tbsp black gram (urad dal), washed
1 tsp rice, washed
3 dry red chillies
½ tsp turmeric powder
Salt to taste
½ coconut, grated
2 tsp cumin seeds

For tempering:

1 tsp brown mustard seeds
1 dry red chilli, broken
1 sprig curry leaves

- Clean and wash toor dal and drain.
- Pressure cook the dal with 2 cups water for 15 minutes.
- While dal is cooking, put oil in a kadhai and sauté for 2 minutes all the ingredients for the paste and blend.
- To the cooked dal add snake gourd and salt to taste. Add 1 cup water. Cook for 10 minutes or until snake gourd is tender.
- Now add paste and mix. Cook for 5 minutes and set aside. Heat oil in a small kadhai and add mustard seeds, chilli and curry leaves. When seeds pop, add to the stew and cover. Serve hot with rice.

JHINGE POSHTO

Ridge Gourd with Poppy Seeds

Serves 6

1 kg ridge gourd (jhinge/touri)
Salt to taste
3 tbsp oil
¼ tsp mustard seeds
2 dry red chillies

For paste:

¼ tsp turmeric powder
1 dry red chilli
4 green chillies

For tempering:

1 onion, finely chopped
2 tbsp poppy seeds (khus khus), ground to a paste

- Peel and chop ridge gourd. Add salt and set aside for a while. Remove excess moisture by squeezing. Discard water.

- Heat oil in kadhai and fry mustard seeds and 2 red chillies for 1 minute. Add ridge gourd and fry for 2 minutes over brisk fire. Then cover and cook for 3 minutes on a low fire.

- Grind turmeric, dry chilli and green chillies into a paste, and add to the vegetables with salt.

- Add sliced onion and fry uncovered for 3 minutes.

- Add the poppy-seed paste, stir-fry until the vegetable is quite dry and just turning brown.

- Serve at room temperature.

PAVAKYA PACHADI

Bitter Gourd Salad

Serves 6

1 tsp corn oil
2 onions, sliced lengthwise
250 gm bitter gourd, finely chopped
1 tsp chilli powder
1 tbsp jaggery
1½ cups curd
Salt to taste

For tempering:
1 tsp black gram (urad dal), washed
½ tsp corn oil
1 tsp brown mustard seeds
2 dry red chillies, broken
1 sprig curry leaves

- Heat oil in a kadhai. Add onions and fry till transparent. Add bitter gourd and fry till crisp.

- Add chilli and jaggery to ¼ cup water in a pan. Simmer covered for 3 minutes.

- Beat the curd till smooth and add bitter gourd mixture with salt to taste.

- For tempering, heat oil in a kadhai, add urad dal and stir for half a minute. Add the rest of the ingredients and mix. When the mustard seeds pop, add to the curd mixture. Mix well and serve at room temperature.

- Serve as a side dish with rice, dal and vegetables.

cabbage

Cabbage is anathema to those of us who have been in boarding schools or have lived in paying guest accommodations in England. Cabbage used to grow wild in northern England and were bitter, yet were the only source of greens. It was the Romans, it appears, who introduced cultivated variety which was not so bitter.

A holiday spent by acquaintances in Ireland was full of anecdotes about the strange smell of boiled cabbage which dominated the township, and their attempts to escape it. The conclusion drawn was that it was the smell of boiled cabbage that made the inhabitants take to whisky.

In fact, not only in Europe, but in other parts of the world such as China and Korea, cabbage is the only green vegetable available during the long winter months. I happened to be in North Korea when it was *kimchee* time. The entire transportation system was commandeered for distributing the Chinese cabbage throughout the country. Wherever I went I heard the pounding of chillies and saw operation *kimchee* in progress. This tradition has been maintained by the North Koreans even in Central Asia where they were settled in the thirties by Stalin. The pickled *kimchee* is an important commodity even in remote village bazaars. It is a life saver for Indians who work in Central Asia and are starved for the taste of vegetables and spice.

Personally, I love a crisp salad of cabbage or the quick stir-fried concoction which we call *kachi pakki*—raw and cooked and stuffed cabbage leaf or dolmas. I also devised my own quick borsch made from canned tomato juice and cabbage with a dollop of thickened yogurt and red pepper. Then there is the stuffed cabbage which is slightly tricky to make but quite delicious.

Why is it that all the vegetables which are good for us bring memories that are off-putting? Cabbage is an excellent vegetable which provides us with fibres and with minerals. Cabbage is also reputed to deter cancer. So it is important to overcome one's inhibitions and convince the palate that here is a versatile vegetable that is not only good, but is also easy to cook and delicious.

CABBAGE SALAD

Serves 4

¼ cup boiling water
1 cabbage head, finely shredded
¼ tsp salt
1 large carrot, peeled and finely grated
1 capsicum, very finely sliced
Juice of 1 small lime
¼ cup fresh green coriander
1 cup mayonnaise

- Pour boiling water over shredded cabbage and sprinkle salt.

- Knead the cabbage to soften, after which squeeze out all the water.

- Add carrot and capsicum, lime juice, coriander and mayonnaise.

- Mix thoroughly and refrigerate.

- This can be kept for days in the refrigerator and served as a side dish.

CABBAGE AND WALNUT
SALAD

Serves 4

500 gm cabbage, finely shredded
2 celery sticks, coarsely chopped
1 large onion, finely chopped
1 tart green apple, coarsely chopped
½ cup walnuts, coarsely crushed
½ cup French dressing

· Mix all the ingredients together.

· Check the taste, and if necessary add more dressing.

· This is an excellent salad to eat for cabbage is the best
source of fibre.

JASLEEN'S KIMCHEE

1 kg Chinese cabbage or inner part of ordinary cabbage
2 tbsp salt
2 green apples, cut into thin strips
6 spring onions, chopped
1" piece ginger, ground
10 cloves garlic, ground
1 tbsp sesame seeds, roasted and ground
1 tbsp chilli powder
1 tbsp powdered jaggery
3 tbsp vinegar
3 tbsp soya sauce

- Separate cabbage leaves and wash well. Drain. Dry on a towel.

- Hold a bunch of cabbage leaves together and chop into 1" pieces.

- Place in a bowl and sprinkle salt. Toss periodically for 4 hours. If using ordinary cabbage, crush with the hand and squeeze out excess moisture.

- Add apples and spring onions and mix together, preferably using your hands so that the moisture and salt blend well.

- Add the rest of the ingredients and mix well.

- Spoon into a jar, pouring the liquid on top. Close the lid. Keep in sun for 2 days, shaking the bottle often.

- Refrigerate. Serve as a side dish.

- The kimchee will keep for 7 to 10 days in the refrigerator.

KACHI PAKKI

Stir-fried Cabbage

Serves 6

1 large cabbage, 750 gm-1 kg
5 green chillies
3 tbsp oil
2 dry red chillies
1 pinch asafoetida powder
1 tsp cumin seeds
½ tsp mustard seeds
¼ tsp fenugreek seeds
¼ tsp turmeric powder
1 tsp salt
2 tbsp malt vinegar

· Chop cabbage into thin slivers and cut green chillies lengthwise. Set aside.

· Heat oil in a kadhai and allow it to smoke. Remove from fire.

· Add 2 red chillies, asafoetida, cumin, mustard and fenugreek and stir briskly. Replace on fire. Add turmeric. When the seeds begin to pop, add cabbage and green chillies. Sprinkle salt on top.

· Stir cabbage with a lift and shake movement, until the leaves are covered with the oil and spices. Continue to stir for 5 minutes.

· Add vinegar, stir again for a minute and take off the fire.

CABBAGE AND CAPSICUM

- · Use the same ingredients as in the previous recipe. Add 4 capsicums.

- · Cut capsicum in half and remove seeds. Cut into thin, long strips.

- · Follow the previous recipe except in this case, put the capsicums before the cabbage and stir-fry briskly for 2 minutes. Continue the recipe from here.

DOLMA: STUFFED
CABBAGE LEAVES

Serves 6

10 cabbage leaves
1 cup home-made cottage cheese (paneer)
2 onions, chopped
4 walnuts, crushed
1 bunch mint, finely chopped
2 tbsp cumin seeds, roasted
½ tsp chilli powder
1 tsp salt
1 tsp butter
1 cup tomato sauce (p.339)

· Put a large pan of water to boil. Cut the top of a large cabbage to expose inner leaves. Hold cabbage by its stem and plunge into water for 5 minutes. Remove using a skimmer or a metal colander. Cool and remove as many leaves as you can easily. Repeat until you have the amount needed.

· Cut the central thick part of the large leaf, dividing into half, and retain the smaller ones whole.

· Drain and dry with a clean towel and set aside.

· Mix together paneer, onions walnut, mint, cumin, chilli powder and salt.

· Divide the mixture into the number of dolmas you wish to make—preferably 14 to 16.

· Select leaf and place the filling ⅓ of the way from one end, spreading it horizontally. Fold leaf up to cover and tuck in the sides to contain filling. Gently roll it across. Use a toothpick to hold it together.

· Butter a baking dish and place the rolls of cabbage. Cover top with foil.

· Add tomato sauce. Cook for 20 minutes in a moderate oven at 250°C.

· Remove foil and bake for another 5 minutes and serve.

VEGETARIAN BORSCH

Serves 6

500 gm cabbage
1 kg tomatoes
200 gm carrot, thinly sliced
250 gm pumpkin, skinned and cut into small pieces
6 cloves garlic, finely sliced
1 green chilli, sliced
3 vegetable bouillon cubes
1 tsp salt
1 tbsp lime juice
1 cup curd
⅛ tsp chilli powder/paprika
2 leaves of lemon grass tied in a knot (optional)

· Divide cabbage in half and cut into thin strips. Wash thoroughly and drain in colander.

· Put tomatoes in boiling water, skin and chop.

· Put two cups of water in a large pan and add vegetarian bouillon cubes and lemon grass.

· As the water begins to boil, add all the ingredients except cabbage. Cool and run through liquidizer. Return to the pan.

· Before serving dinner, add 3 cups water, salt and lime juice to the pan and heat. As it boils, put in the cabbage, cover and allow to come to a boil. Cook for 5 minutes. Drain. Discard the water and add cabbage to the soup and cook together till it comes to a boil. Lower flame and simmer for 5 minutes.

- Whip curd till smooth.
- Pour soup into serving bowl. Pour the curd on top and sprinkle red chilli or paprika on top. Serve immediately.

An instant way to make this soup is to use 2 tins of tomato soup. Heat the soup with crushed garlic, salt and pepper, add water to thin the consistency. When it boils, add the chopped cabbage. Boil together and serve with curd and paprika.

c a r r o t

Carrots have come a full circle. They originally came to us from the mountains of Afghanistan. They were purple in colour and succulent. Today, they have retained their succulence, but are orange in colour. The original purple carrots are rare and used for making the delicious, slightly fermented sour drink *kanji*, which is a favourite winter drink for Punjabis. The carrot went to Europe via Spain, where it was taken by the conquering Islamic armies. It was seen as an exotic vegetable and its feather-like leaves were often used as plumage in place of feathers.

Children usually abhor carrots. They have been fed carrots mushy, boiled and mashed and never as they should be eaten—grated or semi-raw, with all the goodness of life in them.

When new vegetables began to be available in the markets in India in the sixties, a pale version of the carrot began to be sold as *angrezi gaajar* for twice the price of the *desi*. The *desi* one was a bright orange, not so elegantly tapered, and full of whiskers, but was succulent and delicious when eaten. Plumage apart, the way I like to eat carrots is raw or in the most wonderful and delectable of all dishes, the carrot halwa, soaking with ghee, solidified cream of milk and full of nuts, sinful but delicious!

71

However, I don't have the recipe here, since it's easy enough to find and is carried in many excellent Indian cookbooks. My aim is to make cooking easy, healthy yet tasty, so that you can wake up next morning without groaning with indigestion. Carrots are full of Vitamins A and D. They are good for your eyesight and are now prescribed even by allopathic doctors. A French friend, Michelle, developed eye problems which made her life miserable, and was prescribed carrots with each meal by her doctor. Being French and a great lover of food, she felt that she would soon reincarnate as a rabbit. I happened to be in Paris then and she fell on my neck crying: Jasleen, I hate carrots. What can I do? I told her: Come to love them of course, and prepared for her a carrot meal.

Bless the supermarkets. I got grated carrots in a packet. Carrots cut in roundels and carrots cut in sticks. I made a carrot salad (see recipe on p. 75), cooked carrots with dried fenugreek leaves (see recipe on p. 79), carrot sticks cut in half and cooked with home-made cheese. A grilled fish, of course, to go with it, with a carrot dessert (see recipe on p.350) in addition. The meal was complete. She and her husband loved it and were immediately converted to carrot therapy. My charming, sophisticated French host, Phillipe Vaz, whose kitchen had been the scene of the cooking, said at the end of the meal: 'It was delicious, but I do feel like a gourmet rabbit. I have learnt today never to challenge Jasleen, otherwise I may be consuming pumpkins all my life and be reborn as one.'

CORAL AND EMERALD DELIGHT

Serves 6

500 gm carrots
8 cloves garlic, crushed
1 level tsp salt
½ tsp chilli powder
2 leaves of lemon grass tied in a knot
4 tbsp fresh lime juice
2 tbsp chopped basil or mint

· Wash, scrape, chop and boil carrots in 4 cups water with crushed garlic, salt, sugar, chilli powder and lemon grass.

· When done, remove from fire. Cool, remove lemon grass and purée, adding lime juice.

· Add water to give it the consistency of soup.

· Before serving, taste the soup and correct seasoning. Add mint or basil.

· This soup can be served hot or cold (in summer) with a cube of ice.

CARROT AND ORANGE SOUP

Serves 6

1 kg carrots
5 cloves garlic, finely sliced
2 leaves of lemon grass tied in a knot
2 cups fresh orange juice or medium pack of orange juice
2 tbsp lime juice
½ tsp salt
¼ tsp chilli powder (optional)
2 tsp chopped basil or mint leaves

- Wash and scrape carrots and chop coarsely.

- Put 5 cups water to boil and add carrots, garlic and lemon grass. Cook for 15 to 20 minutes until the carrots are soft.

- Strain the mixture, reserving the liquid. Discard lemon grass.

- Pureé mixture, adding orange juice, lime juice, salt and chilli powder.

- You can serve this soup hot or cold. Before serving, add the basil or mint leaves.

GRATED CARROT SALAD

Serves 6

1 kg carrot, grated
50 gm green coriander, chopped
2 tbsp lime juice
1 tbsp corn oil
½ tsp salt
½ tsp mustard seeds
6 to 7 outer lettuce leaves

· Put grated carrots and coriander in a bowl.

· Mix together rest of the ingredients, add to salad and mix well.

· Line the salad bowl with washed and dried lettuce leaves and arrange the salad on top.

· Chill before serving.

GAAJAR KACHUMBAR

Carrot Grated

Serves 6

6 carrots, peeled and grated
1 large onion or 2 spring onions along with leaves, finely chopped
100 gm mint leaves, chopped
1 tbsp raisins, washed and soaked in water
2 tbsp lime juice
Salt and pepper to taste

- Mix carrots with onion, mint and raisins. Toss together with lime juice, salt and pepper.

- Refrigerate for 1 hour before serving.

CARROT AND COTTAGE CHEESE SALAD

Serves 6

500 gm thin, long carrots
1 tsp salt
1 cup home-made cottage cheese (paneer)
2 tbsp chopped green coriander

· Peel carrots and cut in ¼" roundels.

· Put sufficient water to immerse all the carrots or do it in batches. Add 1 tsp salt. When water begins to boil, add the carrots. As soon as the water begins to boil again, remove carrots from the water and drain.

· Cool the carrots and mix with 1 cup paneer and 1 tbsp green coriander.

· Garnish with the remaining green coriander and serve.

CARROT SALAD WITH SESAME SEEDS

Serves 4

500 gm carrots
2 tbsp chopped mint or coriander
1½ tbsp sesame seeds, roasted
½ cup French dressing
½ tsp chilli powder (optional)

- Scrape and cut carrots in thin roundels.

- Put into boiling water and strain immediately after the water begins to boil.

- Mix the carrots, mint or coriander and 1 tbsp sesame seeds.

- Mix French dressing with chilli powder and blend well.

- Place salad in a dish and sprinkle the remaining sesame seeds on top.

GAAJAR METHI

Carrots and Dried Fenugreek

Serves 6

2 tbsp oil
2 dry red chillies
4 tbsp dried fenugreek leaves, soaked in a cup of water
1 kg carrot, cleaned and cut in thin roundels
½ tsp chilli powder (optional)
1 tsp salt
1 heaped tsp dried mango powder (amchur)

- Heat oil in a kadhai until it begins to smoke.
- Add whole chillies and stir for less than half a minute.
- Remove from fire.
- Add fenugreek to oil after squeezing out water.
- Return to fire and sauté for 1 minute.
- Add carrots and remaining spices and stir briskly for 2 minutes or so until the carrots are completely mixed with oil, fenugreek and spices.
- Sprinkle water on the carrots, lower flame and cook covered for 10 minutes, stirring periodically.
- Remove lid and stir-fry on medium fire until the moisture is absorbed and the fenugreek looks crisp.
- Serve hot with chapatti, curd and chutney.

In summer eating bitter vegetables like fenugreek and bitter gourd is essential for a healthy digestive system. In

fact, among Bengalis the meal begins with a bitter
vegetable to stimulate the body's digestive juices.

GAAJAR AUR PANEER

Carrots with Cottage Cheese

Serves 6

1 kg carrots, cut in ½" thick roundels
2 tsp mustard oil
1 tsp cumin seeds
½ tsp turmeric powder
½ tsp chilli powder
1 cup crushed cottage cheese (paneer)
1 spring onion, finely chopped
1 green chilli, finely chopped
2 tbsp chopped green coriander
1 tsp salt

- Put carrots in boiling water. When the water begins to boil again, remove and drain.

- Heat oil in a kadhai until it smokes.

- Add cumin seeds and sauté for half a minute, then add carrots and sauté briskly for 1 minute.

- Add turmeric powder and sauté for half a minute, then add chilli powder.

- Mix cottage cheese with spring onion and add to carrots. Add green chilli and coriander. Add salt and stir together until completely mixed. Remove from heat and serve.

This dish not only tastes good, but also looks beautiful. The combination of orange, white and green with flecks of black is most attractive.

c a u l i f l o w e r

Cauliflower or phool gobi, is the Indian word for flowering cabbage. The white, closely knit florets surrounded by green leaves look beautiful growing in rows in the garden. I plant cornflowers behind the cauliflower beds.

Cauliflower is supposed to have come from the Arab world. Some say it was brought by the Crusaders to Europe, others think it was brought by the Moors to Spain. A range of dishes in different parts of the world have made it part of the cuisine of different cultures. Mark Twain's description of cauliflower is rather quaint, 'a cabbage with a college education'. Since I am partial to cauliflower, I would like to add my description, 'a delightful edible bouquet of flowers.'

I never throw away any part of it. I learnt to do this in New York where it cost a bomb. I remove the flowering head and set it aside to be cooked whole or in separate florets. I cut off the leaves and their stems and even use the thick coarse stems which I cook separately, like chewy vegetarian bones. The stems and leaves make an excellent vegetable with the stem slit through the middle and cut ½" in width and 2" in length. The central portion is soft while the outer stem is juicy and fibrous inside.

CAULIFLOWER SALAD
Serves 4

500 gm cauliflower, separated into florets
3 spring onions, finely chopped
1 tbsp white sesame seeds, roasted
1 tsp black cumin seeds, roasted
½ tsp chilli sauce
½ cup French dressing

· Boil water in pan and put in cauliflower florets. Drain after 5 minutes. Keep in colander for 15 minutes, tossing until the water is completely drained out.

· Add spring onions.

· Powder white sesame seeds, reserving one-eighth for garnishing.

· Blend black sesame seeds with sesame paste, chilli sauce and French dressing. Pour over the vegetables, mixing well together.

· Sprinkle the remaining sesame over the salad and refrigerate.

CAULIFLOWER AND GREEN BEANS SALAD

Serves 6

1 cauliflower (approx. 500 gm), separated into florets
300 gm French beans strung and chopped (approx. ½" in width)
¾ cup French dressing
2 tbsp lime juice
1 tbsp sesame seeds, roasted
1 tsp chilli sauce
Salt to taste

- Wash cauliflower florets and plunge into boiling water. Remove after 5 minutes and drain.

- String and cut beans into ½" pieces, and plunge into boiling water. Remove after 10 minutes and drain. Both vegetables must be crisp.

- Mix together with dressing, lime juice, sesame seeds, chilli sauce and salt.

- Serve at room temperature.

CAULIFLOWER WITH PARMESAN

Serves 4

1 cauliflower, approx. 750 gm
3 heaped tbsp grated Parmesan
Salt and pepper to taste
1 tbsp oil
1 tbsp butter

· Remove head of cauliflower, wash thoroughly and drain. Put in a pot of salt water for half an hour which will get rid of any insects that may be inside.

· Put 2 cups of water to boil and add 1 tsp salt. Lower the cauliflower after cutting a cross at the base of the stem. Cook in a covered pan for 10 minutes or until the stem is soft but not soggy. Remove from water.

· Mix 2 tbsp Parmesan with salt and pepper and three-quarters of the oil. Place the cauliflower on its head and apply the paste on its underside.

· Place the cauliflower top side up in an oiled, rounded dish. Apply butter. Sprinkle with dry Parmesan cheese.

· Grill until cheese melts and turns brown.

· Serve hot.

RED HOT CAULIFLOWER

Serves 6

1 kg cauliflower
2 tbsp butter
8 cloves garlic, crushed
2 dry red chillies, ground in a pestle
¼ tsp salt
2 tbsp oil

- Separate cauliflower into florets.

- Plunge into boiling water for 5 minutes and drain.

- Melt butter in a heavy frying pan. Add garlic and chillies and sauté for 1 minute. Add florets. Add the oil and salt and mix well. Sauté for 2/3 minutes.

- Add ½ cup water, cover and cook for 5 minutes on low heat.

- Serve hot with rice or noodles.

GOBI ALU

Cauliflower and Potatoes

Serves 6

2 tbsp oil
1 pinch asafoetida powder
1 cauliflower (approx. 750 gm), separated into florets
500 gm potatoes, boiled, peeled and cubed
1 tsp coriander powder
1 tsp cumin powder
½ tsp turmeric powder
¼ tsp chilli powder
½ tsp salt

· In a kadhai heat oil, add a pinch of asafoetida. Add vegetables and sprinkle all the spices.

· Sauté together for 2 to 3 minutes.

· Cover, lower heat and cook for 3 minutes.

· Stir and sprinkle water and cook until the vegetables are done.

GOBI MATAR SABZI

Cauliflower with Peas

Serves 6

2 tbsp oil
2 dry red chillies
1 pinch asafoetida powder
1 cauliflower (approx. 1 kg), separated into florets
½ tsp coriander powder
½ tsp cumin powder
¼ tsp turmeric powder
¼ tsp chilli powder
2 cups shelled peas
1" piece ginger, chopped

- Heat oil in kadhai, add dry red chillies and asafoetida. Stir for 2 seconds.

- Add cauliflower florets and stir-fry until lightly browned.

- Sprinkle water with fingers and add spices. Cover and lower flame. Cook for 3 minutes.

- Add peas and stir together, add ¼ cup water and cover. Cook for 5 minutes. Stir until vegetables are cooked.

- Remove lid and stir gently so as not to break the florets. Cook till dry. Add ginger.

- Serve hot with chapatti or naan.

PHOOL KOPI SARSON

Cauliflower with Mustard

Serves 4

4 tbsp mustard oil
¼ tsp onion seeds (kalonji)
1 cauliflower (approx. 1 kg), separated into small florets
1 tsp turmeric powder
4-6 tbsp mustard powder
6-10 green chillies, slit
Salt to taste

- Heat oil in pan, add onion seeds, then add cauliflower and fry until lightly brown.

- In 1 cup water, mix turmeric and mustard. Pour into pan through a fine sieve.

- Add green chillies and salt.

- Reduce heat, cook over medium flame until practically dry.

- Remove from heat and serve hot.

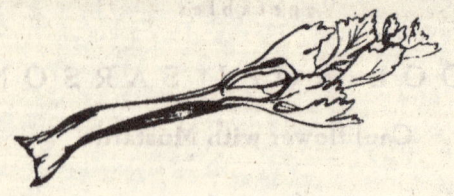

celery

Celery is not an Indian vegetable and has only recently come onto our vegetable lists. It remains an expensive vegetable and is nothing like the wonderful, pale-green celery one gets abroad. Yet it has a delicious flavour and is ideal for soups and salads.

Originally, celery was a medicinal herb, bitter in taste. It was only later that the vegetable gardens developed the celery as we know it today, crisp, succulent and delicious.

I have a neat trick with the celery. I buy a healthy celery with the roots, cut 1" above the roots and plant the celery in a prepared pot. After a few days it begins to sprout and I snip off the leaves to add to soups and salads.

My favourite cooked dish is a Persian delicacy that I learnt from my friend, Parwane Etamadi, who is not only a great painter but also a wonderful cook. I only add some spices which, according to Parwane, lend flavour to it.

TRAVELLER'S SOUP

Syrian Celery Soup

Serves 6

3 vegetable bouillon cubes
6 cloves garlic, crushed
2 potatoes
1 heaped tbsp rice
1 stick celery
1 carrot
3 zucchini or 6 tindas or 500 gm bottle gourd
Salt to taste
2 tbsp lime juice
1 bunch mint

- Heat 8 cups of water, bouillon cubes and crushed garlic in a heavy pan. Peel and dice potatoes and add to the pot along with rice.
- Chop outer long stems of celery with quarter of the leaves and add.
- Cut carrot in thin roundels and add.
- Cook for 7 minutes.
- Add 3 zucchini cut in roundels.
- Add salt and cover.
- Cook for 5 minutes and check if potatoes are done.
- Finely chop the inner celery with leaves and add to soup along with lime juice.
- Chop mint. Reserve 1 tbsp, add rest to the pot. Cover

and cook for 2 minutes.

· Serve the soup hot, adding lime juice and the remaining mint.

This excellent soup, usually made with chicken, is a complete light meal in itself. My friend Elsie, whose grandparents came from Syria, made it for me whenever I arrived in New York on a visit. The fresh taste of celery and mint with a lemony tang, and its beautiful colours, make it ideal after a long journey. One can serve it with toasted bread, naan or Lebanese bread and mixed salad.

CELERY DELIGHT
Serves 4

1 large bunch celery
3 large onions
2 tbsp olive oil or Saffola
2 dry red chillies
1 tsp cumin seeds, roasted
2 heaped tsp sugar
1 tsp salt
3 tbsp lime juice

- Separate celery leaves and wash carefully. Separate the stems from the leaves. Use only half the leaves from the inner stems, the rest can be used for other dishes.

- Cut the stems into 1½" long pieces and chop up the leaves.

- Cut onions lengthwise.

- Put oil in a kadhai and heat. Add red chillies and cumin and fry for half a minute.

- Add onions and stir-fry until they are transparent and give out an aroma.

- Add celery and stir-fry for 5 minutes.

- Add sugar, salt and ½ cup water. Cook covered for 10 minutes, until celery is cooked yet crisp.

- Add lime juice and stir. Serve hot.

Optional garnish:
¾ cup curd or yoghurt, beaten smooth

¼ tsp salt
¼ tsp powdered sugar
¼ tsp saffron

· In a bowl put 3 tbsp curd, salt and sugar. Add saffron and beat together, rubbing in the saffron to release its colour.

· Add the rest of the curd and stir it all together.

· Keep in refrigerator overnight.

· Pour over the celery before serving.

This is a very delicate dish of Persian origin which is traditionally cooked with lamb.

CELERY WALDORF SALAD

Serves 6

1 bunch celery
500 gm tart green apples
½ cup walnuts
¼ cup French dressing
¼ cup mayonnaise
1 tbsp lime juice

· Separate celery stems and discard the outer leaves. Wash and slice thinly into ¼" wide pieces.

· Cut unpeeled apples into thin slices and halve them.

· Reserve six halves of walnuts and crush others coarsely.

· Mix all the ingredients together. Taste, and if necessary add more dressing.

· Pour into a bowl and decorate with walnuts.

· Chill before serving.

CELERY AND GREEN
PAPAYA SALAD

Serves 6

½ bunch celery
500 gm green papaya
¼ cup minced mint leaves
¼ cup peanuts
2 tsp soya sauce
2 tsp malt vinegar
1 dry red chilli, powdered
½ tsp salt

- Prepare celery as for Celery Waldorf Salad (p. 95).

- Skin the papaya and slice. Put in salt water for half an hour.

- Drain and grate. Put in water for half an hour. Drain and then dry on a towel.

- Mix papaya and celery together with mint.

- Roast peanuts on a griddle, remove skins and crush coarsely in a pestle.

- Mix soya sauce, vinegar, chilli and salt and pour over the salad.

- Add crushed peanuts, reserving 1 tbsp.

- Mix together. Transfer to a bowl and sprinkle with remaining peanuts on top.

- Refrigerate for at least half an hour.

CELERY SALAD DIVINE

Serves 6

1 bunch celery
3 potatoes, boiled, peeled and cubed
1 onion, finely chopped
12 olives
¼ cup chopped mint
½ cup French dressing
1 tsp lime juice
½ tsp salt

· Prepare celery as for Celery Waldorf Salad (p. 95).

· Mix with hot potatoes, onion and mint.

· Add French dressing, lime juice and salt and mix.

· Taste to correct seasoning.

· Refrigerate before serving.

CELERY WITH VEGETABLES

Serves 6

1 medium-sized stick celery
2 large onions
3-5 green chillies
2 carrots
1 zucchini
300 gm sprouted beans
2 tbsp olive oil or Saffola
2 dry red chillies
1 tsp salt
1 tsp sugar
1 tbsp light soya sauce
½ tsp chilli sauce
3 tbsp lime juice
10 basil leaves

· Wash celery and remove outer leaves. Cut into ½" pieces. Cut the onions lengthwise. Slit green chillies and deseed.

· Cut carrots in thin roundels.

· Cut zucchini in ¼" thick roundels.

· Wash sprouted beans in water, drain and set aside.

· Heat oil in a kadhai and add dry chillies, sauté for half a minute.

· Add onion and sauté until transparent.

· Add carrot and sauté for 1 minute.

· Add the celery and stir-fry for 5 minutes.

- Add zucchini and green chillies, stir all together for 2 minutes.

- Now sprinkle salt, sugar, soya sauce, chilli sauce and lime juice and stir together.

- Sprinkle water generously and cover. Lower flame and cook for 5 minutes.

- Remove lid and add sprouted beans and basil leaves. Stir briskly, taking care not to break any vegetables.

- Check for salt, and if necessary add more salt and lime juice.

- **Serve hot.**

c u c u m b e r

The delicious cucumber rests between being a vegetable and a fruit. In Iran, nobody cooks it. It is served along with fruit. Whenever we went to a Persian party, we were served huge trays of beautifully arranged fruit. Tangerines and oranges, plums and apricots, depending on the season, and small green cucumbers. The men and women peeled the fruit elegantly. The apples and oranges were peeled in a circular manner. The skin of cucumbers fell away from them like peeled bananas. In no time the trays laden with fruit would be empty and the plates would be filled with mounds of peels.

There is nothing more delicious than small, succulent cucumbers on a hot summer's day. I was told a delightful story by my archaeologist friend, David Stronach: Ur-Namnu, who lived in Mesopotamia 4,000 years ago, relished cucumbers so much that he had a temple built to Naanna to protect his gardens. Another historian capped the story by relating how the Roman Emperor Tiberius was so fond of cucumbers that he raised them on wheels, so that they could be protected from the cold and also be brought fresh to his table during his campaigns.

Cucumbers are known today to be an excellent diuretic and also contain certain basic minerals which the body needs. A number of nature care diets prescribe cucumber juice.

The best way to have cucumbers is raw, in salads, in sandwiches and also in a favourite soup of mine which I first had in Bangkok at the home of Sarojini Vittachi, when I was visiting her. I have modified the recipe, and instead of making it with chicken, I use paneer and mint. Believe me, the paneer recipe is more delicious and easier to make.

CUCUMBER AND COTTAGE CHEESE SOUP

Serves 6

3 cucumbers, 8" long
200 gm cottage cheese (paneer)
100 gm green coriander, chopped
1 tsp salt
3 leaves of lemon grass
2 tbsp lime juice

- Peel cucumbers and taste for bitterness. Discard bitter cucumbers. Cut both ends and set aside.

- Hollow out the inside, removing all the seeds and set aside.

- Take 200 gm paneer, mash it well, mix with 50 gm coriander, ½ tsp salt and stuff the cucumbers.

- Close both ends with the pieces set aside earlier, using wooden toothpicks.

- Put cucumbers flat into a pot and add 7 cups water, lemon grass and remaining salt. Add the remaining paneer stuffing as well as the remaining coriander.

- Cook covered on slow fire for 10 to 15 minutes. Test with a fork to see if the cucumbers are done. Remove from fire. Add lime juice.

- Take the cucumbers from the pot and remove the ends. Cut the cucumbers into four pieces. Put two pieces in each bowl and ladle soup on top.

- This soup should be served hot.

This soup is based on a Thai soup made with cucumber and chopped chicken. It has been made into a vegetarian soup by putting paneer and coriander leaves and thickened by adding bits of the stuffing. It is a light soup and an appetizing way to begin a meal. It also has a very delicate appearance. The translucent jade of the cucumber, the white paneer pieces and dark green flecks of coriander are reminiscent of the *houldili* pendants of jade inlaid with emeralds which were worn by women in the North West Frontier Province, the land of my ancestors.

COLD CUCUMBER SOUP

Serves 6

3 cucumbers, 8" long
2 tbsp soya sauce
1 tsp chilli sauce
1 tbsp sesame seeds, roasted and ground
½ tsp sugar, powdered
1 tsp salt
3 tbsp lime juice
5 cups vegetable stock
4 spring onions, finely chopped
1 bunch coriander leaves, finely chopped

- Peel and slice cucumbers thinly and taste for bitterness. Discard bitter cucumbers. Add all the ingredients except stock, spring onions and coriander, and mix well. Let it stand for 1 hour, stirring constantly.

- Add stock, spring onions and coriander and chill soup.

- Serve the soup ice-cold.

CUCUMBER AND CURD SUMMER SOUP

Serves 6

1 kg curd
3 cucumbers, 8" long
1 large onion
1 bunch fresh mint, finely chopped
4 walnuts, chopped
2 tbsp raisins
1 tsp salt
½ tsp black pepper

- Mix curd to a smooth cream.

- Peel cucumbers and check for bitterness. Discard if bitter. Cut sweet cucumbers into bite-size pieces.

- Mince onion and mix with mint leaves and walnuts.

- Add water slowly, mixing everything. The consistency should be that of soup or a thin batter.

- Refrigerate for at least 2 hours.

- Wash raisins and soak in water.

- Before serving, add raisins, salt and pepper.

- Mix well and serve.

- Do not add salt earlier as it will make the soup watery.

This is served in Iran as a summer soup.

An interesting way to serve it is to place it on the table

surrounded by small bowls of all the ingredients and to let people make their own blend of flavours.

CUCUMBER DELIGHTS

A wonderful way to serve cucumbers as a side dish is to hollow them out and cut into 2" barrel shapes. Place the barrels on individual salad leaves and fill them up with any of the following:

Guacamole (See recipe on p. 25)
Hummus (See recipe on p. 275)
Indian Tabbouleh (See recipe on p. 303)

CUCUMBER AND PEANUT SALAD

Serves 6

4 cucumbers
1 onion, finely chopped
½ tsp chilli powder
1 tbsp soya sauce
1 tbsp malt vinegar
1 tsp salt
3 tbsp peanuts, freshly roasted and skinned

- Peel the cucumbers. Taste to check for bitterness. If bitter, discard.

- Run the fork tines down the side of each cucumber to make grooves.

- Chop in thin roundels.

- Add the remaining ingredients, reserving 1 tsp chopped peanuts. Refrigerate.

- Before serving, arrange cucumbers in a flat dish. Pour the sauce on top. Sprinkle peanuts and serve.

COOKED CUCUMBER SALAD

Serves 4

250 gm cucumbers
1 tsp salt
2 tsp hot sesame oil
3 spring onions, chopped
1 tbsp soya sauce
1 tbsp malt vinegar
1 tsp sugar
1 tsp chilli powder
1 tbsp sesame seeds, roasted and made into a paste, reserving
a little for garnish

- Peel cucumbers. Check for bitterness. If bitter, discard. Cut into slices, sprinkle ½ tsp salt, mix well and keep in colander for half an hour. Squeeze out excess moisture.

- Heat sesame oil in a frying pan. Add cucumber and spring onion, sauté briskly for a minute.

- Add all ingredients and cook for 2 to 3 minutes. Stir all the while.

- Spoon into a white or glass dish. Sprinkle reserved sesame seeds and serve.

o k r a

I always thought that okra came to India from America until I came across a reference to it in Jane Grigsons' *Vegetable Book,* which said that this vegetable is a native of West Africa and was taken by the slaves to the Americas. Okra is derived from *nakurama,* a word in the Twi language in Ghana. It is also the name of the great leader Nakurama who was the President of the country when Ghana became independent.

Okra used to be put in the sauce for eating *fufu* in Ghana. The pounded yam *fufu* would be served in large platters with a soup of okra and tomatoes; the slippery consistency of the okra would help in eating the slightly dry *fufu*. Much to the delight of my Ghanian friends, I learnt quickly to scoop the *fufu* up with my fingers, dip it in the sticky liquidy sauce, and eat it with ease. I never let on that we Indians anyway eat rice with our fingers.

We in India love the okra and will eat it mostly as a dry vegetable. We cook it so as to prevent the sticky juices from being released. In Turkey they have a special way of preparing okra by rubbing in vinegar and salt. After half an hour, the okra is rinsed and dried, and it does not lose its colour or texture.

OKRA SALAD

Serves 6

250 gm thin, small okra
1 tbsp olive oil
2 tsp lime juice
1 tsp soya sauce
½ tsp salt
¼ tsp black pepper
¼ tsp mustard

· Wash okra well. Cut away the top of the vegetable carefully so as not to expose the inner core.

· In a wide pan boil water and add okra. As soon as the water begins to boil again, lower heat, cook for 5 minutes and strain.

· In an airtight bottle, shake all the other ingredients together until they are well mixed. Pour over the okra and mix with a fork and spoon.

· Arrange in a flat dish and pour the sauce over it.

· Refrigerate for at least 1 hour before serving.

This is a delicious salad which I have improvised and I serve it as a side dish as well as with drinks. I call it the Indian asparagus.

OKRA AND MINT

Serves 6

250 gm small okra
2 tbsp olive oil
2 onions, finely chopped
Salt and pepper to taste
2 tbsp lime juice
3 tbsp chopped fresh mint

- Trim the heads of okra and leave them whole.
- In a frying pan heat oil and add the onion. Sauté until transparent.
- Add okra and sauté for 5 to 7 minutes until just tender.
- Add salt, pepper, lime juice and toss together in the pan.
- Sprinkle mint and mix it in.
- Serve hot.

OKRA WITH TOMATOES

Serves 6

3 tbsp oil
2 large onions, finely chopped
6 cloves garlic, crushed
500 gm young okra
1 tsp coriander powder
1 tsp cumin powder
1 tsp black pepper
1 tsp salt
250 gm tomatoes, peeled and chopped
2 tbsp lime juice

- Heat oil and sauté onion in a frying pan until transparent. Add garlic and sauté for 1 minute.

- Now add okra and the spices and salt and fry until crisp and slightly brown.

- Spread the chopped tomatoes on top. Sprinkle lime juice. Sprinkle a little water with fingers and cover.

- Lower flame and simmer for 7 to 8 minutes, shaking the pan so that the okra does not stick to the bottom. If necessary, add more water.

- Serve hot or cold.

You can vary the dish by adding button mushrooms after the okra and before putting in the tomatoes.

BHINDI SABUT

Whole Okra

Serves 6

500 gm thin, long okra
1 tsp cumin powder
1 tsp coriander powder
1 tsp dried mango powder (amchur)
½ tsp chilli powder
1 tsp salt
4 tbsp oil
2 onions (optional)

- Wash and clean the okra. Cut away the tops and slit the sides.

- Mix all the spices together.

- Force open the slit in the okra and push in the mixed spices.

- Heat oil in a kadhai and add the okra. Fry the okra crisp and serve. This will take approximately 20 minutes.

- Another way to cook it is to add onions to the recipe. Chop 2 onions lengthwise. Heat 2 tsp oil and put in the onion. Add ½ tsp salt and fry till brown. Add the okra at the last stage and cook together.

BHINDI KURKUR

Okra Crisp

Serves 6

500 gm okra
4 tbsp oil
½ tsp cumin seeds
½ tsp coriander powder
Salt and pepper to taste

- Chop okra in thin roundels.
- Heat oil in a kadhai. Add cumin and fry for half a minute.
- Add coriander powder, then okra and stir-fry for 20 minutes or until crisp. Add salt and pepper.
- Serve with khichri or with boiled rice.

SOOKHI BHINDI PIAZ

Dry Okra and Onion

Serves 4

500 gm okra
3 large onions
2 tbsp oil
⅛ tsp asafoetida powder
1 tsp coriander powder
1 tsp cumin powder
½ tsp turmeric powder
1 tsp dried mango powder (amchur)
Salt to taste

· Wash the okra, remove the tops and chop into ⅓ " pieces.

· Cut onions into half and slice thinly.

· Heat oil in a kadhai and add asafoetida. Stir into the oil and add onion immediately. Stir-fry till transparent.

· Add okra and all the spices as well as salt and mix. Fry together for 2 minutes. Cover and continue to cook on low fire for 15 minutes. Check if it is cooked properly.

· Serve hot with chapatti.

BHINDI PACHADI

Okra with Curd

Serves 4

250 gm okra
2 tsp oil
1 tsp mustard seeds
1 tsp cumin seeds
1 dry red chilli
1 tsp black gram (urad dal)
1 tsp Bengal gram (chana dal)
1 sprig curry leaves
Salt to taste
1½ cups curd

- Chop okra fine and set aside.

- Heat oil in a kadhai and add all the spices, dal and curry leaves.

- When the mustard seeds pop, add the okra. Cook on low heat, stirring until okra is done.

- Add salt and stir for another minute. Remove from fire.

- Beat curd till smooth and add to okra. Mix together.

- Serve at room temperature.

This is served as a side dish with rice, sambar, or dal with vegetables.

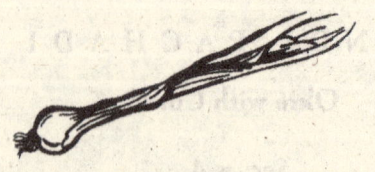

onion and
spring onion

Onions are an indispensable part of any cuisine. I have seen Rajasthani workers on construction sites sitting down to eat their thick *rotlas* with an onion, salt and chillies quickly made into a paste with a little water. Even today one of the most delicious meals for my son and myself is *makkai-ki-roti*, corn chapatti, *sarson-ka-sag*, mustard greens, lentils and a raw onion crushed by hand and fairly shared. The mystique of *mukki-wala-piaz* is only appreciated by Punjabis. The onion is either held in the left hand and given a good blow with the fist or held in one fist and crushed! An eccentric friend, Professor Balbir Singh, could live on crushed onion and fresh chapatti. But the Punjabis are not the only people to like raw onions. Iranians also love eating the delicious *chelo kabab* and *abgosht* with raw onions and herbs.

The onion is one of the oldest cultivated herbs and belongs to the same strain as the fragrant Easter lily. It probably grew wild in the past in Central Asia and was then developed into a cultivable tuber which could be eaten green as well as be used for cooking. The Sanskrit word for the onion is *palandu* and it is referred to in the Puranas. It is believed that onions have been used for more than 6,000 years.

Onions must have been grown and used in Africa too, for it is depicted in Egyptian tombs as early as 3200 BC. In the remote parts of Mali in West Africa, the Dogans, an ancient people with a highly evolved civilization who had been driven away from cultivable valleys to high mountainous areas, cultivated and sold onions as their mainstay. Their weekly markets could be smelt for miles, where onions made into balls were sold to merchants who came from all parts of Mali and even Senegal.

The onion has significant therapeutic qualities. It is considered an excellent antidote to bacteria which may be found in stale food. I remember that when we travelled, my mother always used to carry onions. Any meal that we ate outside the home had to be supplemented by raw onions. Smelling an onion and taking a teaspoon of onion juice would prevent nausea. A cut onion hung under a lamp would drive away mosquitoes. The smell of onion could also keep away suitors!

ONIONS AND TOMATOES

Serves 6

500 gm small onions, the size of walnuts
1 tsp cumin powder
1 tsp coriander powder
½ tsp chilli powder
1½ tsp salt
4 tsp corn oil
6 green chillies
500 gm tomatoes

- Peel the outer skin of the onions and make a cross slit.

- Mix cumin, coriander and chilli powder and ½ tsp of salt and fill the onion slits.

- Put oil in a kadhai and allow it to smoke.

- Remove from the fire, slide in the onions and sauté till they are brown.

- Slit green chillies, deseed and add to the onions.

- Slit tomatoes in half from the top and fill them with the dry masala mixture. Slide them into the kadhai and then work the tomatoes in between onions. Sprinkle remaining salt.

- Cover and cook on slow fire for 8 minutes. Stir with a knife blade so that the tomatoes and onions do not break.

- For serving, lift very gently, so as not to break, on to a flat platter. Pour sauce on top and serve.

This is a dish that I watched my mother make and I always

marvelled at the perfection with which she cooked the vegetables. The glazed onions were a lovely golden brown, while the tomatoes, the love apples, glowed a bright red.

Variation:

ONIONS, TOMATOES AND COTTAGE CHEESE

To the previous recipe add 250 gm cottage cheese (paneer).

- Cut paneer into ¾" by ½" diamonds.
- Heat one tbsp oil in a frying pan, and fry paneer lightly.
- Add fried paneer after the onions and tomatoes are ready, and cook together for 2 minutes.

SPRING ONIONS AND TOFU

Serves 4

3 tbsp corn oil
1 tbsp grated ginger
½ tbsp finely chopped garlic
500 gm spring onions, finely chopped
½ tsp salt
1 tbsp vinegar
250 gm tofu, cut into rectangular pieces
½ tbsp finely chopped green chillies

- Heat oil in a kadhai. Add ginger and garlic and sauté for a minute.

- Add spring onions, sprinkle salt and stir-fry for 5 minutes.

- Add vinegar and stir.

- Then add tofu and green chillies and gently cook for 5 minutes, mixing all the juices together.

- Serve with rice or chapatti.

ROASTED ONIONS

Serves 6

6 large onions
2 tbsp chopped mint
½ tsp salt
3 tbsp vinegar

- Select large onions, place them on the flame over a slotted metal plate or a wire plate until the outer skin is charred.

- Remove outer skin and chop the onion. Add mint, salt and vinegar.

- This is absolutely delicious eaten hot with parantha, hot naan or chapatti.

It can also be eaten cold, as it is, or with yoghurt/curd.

peas

Green peas cooked with paneer, alu and keema are known to be a great delicacy in an Indian kitchen. Personally, I am bored with them. When one travels, which I do all the time, one gets *matar paneer*, *matar alu*, *matar keema* or over-boiled peas, carrots, beans and potatoes until it is coming out of one's ears. I love the taste of fresh peas made in different ways or even eaten raw and remember with nostalgia the taste of the fresh shoots of the pea plant made into a delicious dish in Manipur. I have always tried to grow peas in my garden in place of sweet peas. Though I am not averse to using frozen peas if necessary, personally I prefer the home-grown peas.

Split peas were the staple fare in Europe and in England. I have had a hearty winter soup of split peas cooked with a ham bone. I remember the look of horror on my vegetarian friend's face when she saw the bone emerge on the second day after she had enjoyed bowls of the soup. It reminded me of the nursery rhyme: some like it hot, some like it cold, some like it in the pot, nine days old.

FRESH PEA SOUP

Serves 6

1 kg fresh young peas
Salt to taste
2 tbsp lime juice
10 basil leaves, chopped

· Shell the peas and retain pods.

· In a pot boil 6 cups water. Add the peas and the whole pods and boil for 10 minutes with 1 tsp salt.

· Drain, reserve liquid. Reserve a few young pods and peas and put the rest in a liquidizer and purée.

· Strain through a thin mesh sieve and remove all fibres.

· To the puréed peas add the drained water and the reserved peas and pods.

· Sprinkle lime juice and chopped basil leaves. Serve hot.

SNOW PEAS WITH BUTTER

Serves 6

1 kg fresh snow peas
⅓ cup melted, salty butter
½ tsp salt
2 tbsp lime juice

- Wash peas well.

- Heat a large pot of water. When it begins to boil, add the peas. Cook in boiling water for five minutes. Drain fully, tossing the peas.

- Dry swiftly in a towel and place in a white dish.

- Melt butter and mix with salt and lime juice.

- The dish is now ready to be served. Place a large plate or a soup bowl in front of every person for the discarded pods, and a small bowl for melted butter.

- Pick the peas from the stem. Dip in butter and suck and nibble on the pods.

PEAS À LA PROVENÇAL

Serves 6

8 large salad leaves
2 boiled potatoes, cut in roundels
1 tsp salt
2 large onions, coarsely chopped
3 cups shelled peas
3 tbsp butter
1 tsp black pepper
½ tsp mustard powder

- In a baking dish with cover, arrange salad leaves at the bottom like a nest.
- Line with potatoes and sprinkle a little salt.
- Spread half the chopped onion.
- Mix peas with ½ tsp salt and pour on top. Spread the rest of the onion.
- Melt butter. Add pepper, mustard and remaining salt to ⅓ cup water and melted butter and mix together. Pour over the vegetables.

Cover tightly and cook for 20 to 25 minutes in an oven at medium temperature of 250° C.

Serve in the baking dish.

PULAO OF FRESH PEAS

Serves 6

6 tbsp butter
2 dry red chillies
1 tsp cumin seeds
4 onions, finely chopped
6 cups shelled peas
¼ tsp chilli powder
12 mushrooms, chopped in long strips
1½ tsp salt
2 tsp chopped coriander

- In a kadhai melt 4 spoons butter on low flame. Add dry chillies and cumin and sauté for 1 minute until brown. Add onion and sauté until transparent. Add peas, sprinkle the chilli powder, and toss until everything is mixed together.

- Add 1 cup water and allow it to boil. Lower temperature and simmer covered on a slow fire for 5 minutes. Check that the peas are tender but not too soft.

- Uncover and stir until the water is absorbed.

- Add mushrooms and sauté together, adding the remaining butter. Check for salt.

- Serve with coriander sprinkled on top.

This can be a main dish for those who are allergic to rice or who are on a diet for detoxification.

pepper and capsicum

Capsicums belong to the chilli family and were brought by Christopher Columbus from the Americas. Red peppers are so much a part of the Indian cuisine that we cannot imagine what it must have been like before we knew the use of chilli.

The fiery red chilli—*capsicum frutescenes*—was called pepper by Columbus for he felt that he had discovered a spice to replace black pepper—*piper nigrum*. He also brought the sweet peppers, capsicum, *Capsicumannium*, thus causing a confusion between capsicum, peppers, sweet pepper and chilli. In India we only get one type of capsicum, the bell-shaped sweet peppers. The red and yellow ones are still very rare and are found only in select stores.

Chillies of all varieties are available, from the deadly small red and green ones, to the large red ones which are filled with spices to make pickle. Capsicum and chilli have Vitamin C and are therefore good for us. Many of us cannot eat a meal without a green chilli to bite on.

TARTAR SOUP

Stuffed Capsicum Soup

Serves 6

6 long, green capsicums
200 gm cottage cheese (paneer)
1 heaped tbsp rice
100 gm green coriander or mint, chopped
1 tsp salt
1 tsp black pepper
1 lime

- Cut capsicums around the stems, remove seeds and discard.

- Mix paneer with cleaned and washed rice. Reserve 2 tbsp coriander and add the rest along with ½ tsp salt and ½ tsp black pepper. Mix together.

- Half fill the hollowed capsicums, allowing room for the rice to expand.

- Place the capsicums at the bottom of a pan and add 7 cups water, the rest of the salt and pepper, and any of the paneer mixture left over.

- Allow the water to come to a boil. Lower flame and simmer covered for 12 minutes.

- Add lime juice, sprinkle reserved coriander and serve hot.

This soup is based on a dish made by two sisters who were Tartars and were our hosts in Osh, Kyrgyztan. They had made the soup with capsicums stuffed with mincemeat, rice and herbs. I have improvised by putting in paneer and coriander or mint—whichever is available.

This soup is good for a protein-based menu.

CAPSICUM WITH TOMATOES

Serves 6

6 capsicums
200 gm cottage cheese (paneer)
1 tbsp rice, washed
200 gm green coriander, finely chopped
1 kg tomatoes
1½ tsp salt
1 tsp black pepper
1 tsp cumin, roasted and ground
2 tbsp lime juice

- Cut around the stems of capsicums, remove seeds and discard.

- Mix paneer with rice, two-thirds of the green coriander, ½ tsp salt and ½ tsp pepper.

- Half fill the capsicums with above mixture.

- Lay capsicums flat in a pan.

- Wash tomatoes thoroughly and put into boiling water. Remove from water and peel off the skin.

- Run through liquidizer. Add 1 tsp salt, ½ tsp pepper and cumin.

- Add the tomato juice to the pan.

- Cover and allow the juice to boil. Lower flame and simmer for 15 minutes. Put a metal plate under the pot to prevent any possibility of burning and simmer for another 10 minutes after adding lime juice.

Sprinkle the remaining coriander and serve hot.

This is a variation on the Tartar Soup, and should be served with *rice or chapatti/bread*.

It can also be a light meal served with a big salad and is ideal for a protien-rich diet.

SIMLA MIRCH PORIYAL

Capsicum with Curd

Serves 6

500 gm capsicum
2 tbsp curd
2 tsp oil
1 tsp mustard seeds
1 tsp cumin seeds
¼ tsp asafoetida powder
1 sprig curry leaves
1 tsp garam masala powder
2 tsp grated coconut

· Cut capsicums in roundels and slice each roundel into half. Mix with curd and set aside for half an hour.

· Heat oil in a kadhai and put in all spices except garam masala. Also put in curry leaves.

· When mustard seeds pop, add capsicum and mix thoroughly. Add ¼ cup water.

· Cover and simmer until tender.

· Sprinkle garam masala and coconut. Mix thoroughly and cook for one minute. Remove from fire.

This is delicious with all kinds of food, even a simple vegetarian Western style meal. Can also be served heaped on pieces of crisp toast as a starter.

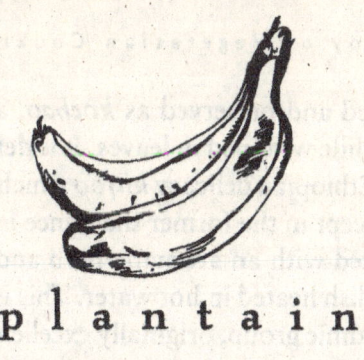

plantain

The banana plant is grown throughout the tropical world, but it is native to Asia. There are several names for the banana in Sanskrit. It is believed that the Greeks, Romans and Arabs praised it greatly. In India a range of bananas are grown, from the large, yellow bananas to red ones, and even tiny, golden ones which are worshipped as phallic symbols. The green variety is eaten cooked, roasted and made into chips.

The banana plant has a high utility value, for every part of it is used for one purpose or the other. The fruit is eaten, the flower made into a speciality vegetable fit for epicures and the leaf is used as a platter or as a wrapper for steaming vegetables and fish, as well as for packing food. The core of the banana is made into a delicious vegetable. The outer peels of the stem can be retted and the fibre that is extracted is used for making twine as well as woven into very fine cloth, which absorbs colours richly. The fruit itself is nutritious and rich in Vitamins A and D.

Ethiopia has a type of tree very similar to the banana plant, the insett, popularly known as the false banana. It has a banana like fruit, which is inedible. The most important segment of this plant is the lower stem which, when cut, provides a variety of food. Its sap is used as gruel, its fibre chopped and preserved as *kochao*, and eaten as bread, baked while wrapped in leaves. It is delicious when eaten with the Ethiopian delicacy *kitfoo* which is similar to steak tartar, except in the former the mince is mixed with hot butter melted with an aromatic herb and served in a black flat clay dish heated in hot water. This is a speciality of the Gruage ethnic group, originally excellent ironsmiths and craftsmen. Some people believe they initially came from India.

PAZHAMPORI

Roasted Plantain

Serves 6

6 large green plantains
6 tbsp liquid palm sugar

· Wrap plantains in foil and place in hot oven at 250°C for 12 minutes or over gas fire for 6 minutes.

· Remove from fire and open it directly on table.

· Place a piece in each plate, slit it open and pour liquid palm gur. Mash and eat.

Liquid palm sugar is a great delicacy in Kerala and West Bengal. It is the dried sap of the juice from the palmyra palm or the date palm. In West Bengal they have a number of delicacies made with the *tad gur* or *khajur gur*.

There is a beautiful poem on the tall palmyra tree by Rabindranath Tagore, which every Bengali child recites with a glint in his eyes, thinking no doubt of the sweet delicacies.

PLANTAIN UPKARI

Raw Green Banana Sautéed

Serves 6

6 large green bananas
1 walnut-sized lump of tamarind, soaked in ½ cup hot water
½ tsp turmeric powder
2 tbsp oil
2 dry red chillies
1 pinch asafoetida powder
1 tsp mustard seeds
1 tsp black gram (urad dal), washed
1 tsp Bengal gram (chana dal), washed
1 tsp cumin seeds
Salt to taste
2 sprigs curry leaves
3 green chillies, slit lengthwise
½ coconut, freshly grated, or 4 tbsp flaked coconut

· Peel bananas and cut into 1" thin roundels.

· In a heavy wok or kadhai place bananas, squeeze out
the juice from tamarind, add turmeric powder and
mix together. Place on a low fire, sprinkling ¼ cup
water over the vegetable and continuing to stir.
Cover and simmer for 5 minutes, then take off fire
and turn gently with spatula to check if the bananas
are cooked. If not cooked, sprinkle water and replace
on fire for 2 minutes more.

· In another pan heat oil, add red chillies and
asafoetida and fry for half a minute. Add all the other
spices, dals, salt and curry leaves, and stir briskly.

- As soon as the mustard seeds begin to pop, add the slit green chillies and stir for a few seconds. Immediately add cooked bananas and grated coconut, stirring them gently with a spatula until the spices and coconut are mixed with the banana. Cook together for one minute.

- Serve with brown rice.

potato

Potatoes are so much a part of the European diet that the town of Offenburg in Germany raised a statue to Sir Francis Drake with a potato in his outstretched hand. He was credited with having brought the potato from the New World. I chuckled when I read this and thought of Sir Francis Drake as an unlikely companion to Lord Ganesha, whose images are seen in many an Indian home with a laddu in his outstretched hand.

Potatoes were greatly maligned in the fifties. They were seen only as sources of carbohydrates, but they were always a favourite dish among all ages and people the world over. Nutritionists have now discovered that they contain vitamins and minerals which are beneficial specially when eaten with the skin intact. As a child, I remember that potatoes were prepared every day in our home, for this was the one dish that everyone would eat with relish. The favourite, of course, was 'Alu Sakrordh', which is a crisp way of making the Indian version of French fries, though with far less oil.

A dish easy to cook and delicious to eat is the egg and potato curry. It is a favourite of my elegant friend, Karen, who is an excellent cook herself. She married a Bengali in London and for her wedding dinner she wanted potato and egg curry. Though her marriage got over a long time ago, her love of curry never diminished. When I was at the University of Minnesota, I would make her the egg curry frequently. She found my recipe non-greasy and lightly spiced yet delicious. The only difference in my cooking in Minneapolis, St. Paul, was that I cheated and used two large teaspoonfuls of condensed tomato paste instead of fresh tomatoes. I don't make this recipe any more since it combines proteins with carbohydrates, but it is nonetheless delicious and quick to prepare.

ALU CHAAT

Indian Potato Salad

Serves 6

2 walnut-sized lumps of tamarind, soaked in hot water
3 tbsp malt vinegar
1½ tsp cumin seeds, freshly roasted and powdered
½ tsp chilli powder
2 green chillies, finely chopped (optional)
6 potatoes, boiled and cut into bite-size pieces
1½ cup white chickpeas, boiled
1½ tsp salt
½ cup fresh pomegranate seeds

- Squeeze out the juice of tamarind and mix with vinegar. Add all the spices, reserving ½ tsp cumin.

- Put potatoes and white chickpeas in the serving bowl. Add the tamarind mixture and mix together.

- Sprinkle the cumin powder on top and follow up with pomegranate seeds.

- This can be eaten as a snack or as part of a meal.

POTATO SALAD WITH SESAME SEEDS

Serves 4

500 gm medium-sized potatoes
2 spring onions, chopped
1½ tbsp sesame seeds, freshly roasted
¾ cup French dressing

· Boil potatoes.

· Peel and cut into bite-size pieces.

· Mix in the spring onions.

· Sprinkle 1 tbsp roasted sesame seeds, reserving the rest.

· Pour the French dressing and mix well.

· Arrange potatoes in a dish for serving. Sprinkle the remaining sesame seeds on top.

ALU SAKRORDH

Crisp Potatoes

Serves 4

2 tbsp oil
2 dry red chillies
6 potatoes, boiled and cut into medium-sized pieces
1 tsp salt
1 tsp coriander seeds

· Put oil in an iron kadhai or heavy non-teflon one and heat until smoking.

· Add chillies and stir for a few seconds.

· Add potatoes and sprinkle salt and coriander seeds on top.

· Stir until the potatoes are coated with oil and seeds are distributed.

· Spread the potatoes as widely as possible at the bottom of the wok.

· Allow the potatoes to stick to the bottom. Use a heavy straight metal spatula with a sharp edge (*khonchi*), scrape the base of the wok until all the potatoes sticking at the bottom have been moved. Stir together and spread potatoes again and repeat the process 2 to 3 times until the potatoes are golden brown and crisp.

KUMAONI ALU TARIWALE

Curried Potatoes from Kumaon

Serves 6

5 potatoes, boiled
2 tbsp oil
¼ tsp chilli powder
1 tsp coriander powder
3 green chillies, slit
½ tsp turmeric powder
2 tomatoes, blanched and chopped
½ cup curd, beaten smooth
1 bunch green coriander

- Cut 4 potatoes into bite-size pieces. Mash the remaining one.

- Heat oil in a heavy-bottomed pan, smoke and remove from fire. When slightly cooled, add potato.

- Add spices and green chillies and stir-fry together until spices are cooked and the aroma of turmeric is released.

- Add tomatoes and stir together for 1 minute.

- Add 2 cups water, stir together and simmer on medium heat for 8 minutes.

- Remove from fire and stir in curd.

- Serve with a sprinkling of green coriander.

BAKED POTATOES

Serves 6

6 medium-sized potatoes
3 tsp butter
6 cloves garlic, ground to a paste
1 tsp mustard
½ tsp salt
½ tsp black pepper

- Roast the potatoes over a gas flame by putting them on a slotted plate or wire frame. Or roast in an oven after cutting each into half with skin intact.

- When the skin is burnt and the potatoes are done, dust off the burnt skin.

- Soften the butter and work in the garlic paste and spices.

- Slit the potatoes and pour in the butter mix.

This dish takes me back to my childhood, when we would sit around a fire and push the potatoes around in the ashes. As we chatted, and listened to stories on the long, cold winter nights, we would burn our fingers as we tried to eat the hot potatoes with the crisp skin, dipping them in salted home-made butter.

ROASTED POTATO SKINS

Serves 4

6 large potatoes
3 tbsp butter
½ tsp salt
½ tsp chilli powder
½ tsp bishop's weed (ajwain)

- Wash potatoes thoroughly.

- Take a sharp knife and cut 2 cm thick slices with skin lengthwise.

- Dip the potato skins in a mixture of butter, salt, chilli powder and ajwain.

- Spread the potato skins with the fleshy part upwards on a buttered plate in an oven and cook for 20 minutes.

- Eat them crisp.

POTATOES AND SESAME SEEDS

Serves 6

3 tbsp oil
2 dry red chillies
6 potatoes, boiled and cut into bite-size pieces
1 tbsp sesame seeds, roasted
1 tsp salt

- Heat oil in a kadhai. As soon as it smokes, drop in red chillies and remove from fire.
- Put in potatoes and ½ tbsp sesame seeds, reserving the rest.
- Sprinkle salt on top.
- Stir-fry for 6 minutes.
- Remove from fire, transfer to serving dish and sprinkle the remaining sesame seeds on top.

ALU TIKIA

Potato Cakes with Basil

Serves 6

½ tsp dried mango powder (amchur)
1 tbsp peanuts, freshly roasted and crushed
½ tsp chilli powder
½ cup basil leaves
4 tbsp oil
2 tsp salt
6 large potatoes, boiled and mashed
3 tbsp milk

· Mix all the ingredients together into a paste except potatoes, milk and 1 tsp salt.

· Add salt and milk to the potatoes and mix to get a paste-like consistency.

· Make a round ball, the size of a golf ball. Hollow out the central part and put in a knob of the basil paste. Cover and flatten into round flat patties.

· On a hot griddle shallow fry the patties until brown on both sides.

POTATO PANCAKES

Serves 4

1 kg potatoes
2 tbsp corn oil
2 tbsp butter
½ tsp salt

- Wash potatoes thoroughly and drain.

- Grate the potatoes with skin.

- Place a non-stick frying pan on fire and put in ¼ tbsp oil, ½ tbsp butter and melt. Grease the pan evenly.

- Spread grated potatoes over the surface approx. ¼" thick and cook. Sprinkle a little oil.

- When cooked on one side, turn over and brown.

- Sprinkle salt and serve hot.

POTATO AND EGG CURRY

Serves 6

3 tbsp oil
6 eggs, hard boiled
2 onions, finely chopped
6 cloves garlic, finely chopped
1 tsp cumin powder
½ tsp chilli powder
½ tsp turmeric powder
3 tomatoes, skinned and chopped
6 potatoes, boiled
1 tsp salt
1 tbsp chopped green coriander

· Heat oil in a pan until it smokes. Take off heat and cool.

· Peel eggs and sauté whole for a minute or two until the skin puckers. Remove with slotted spoon and set aside.

· In the same oil put onion and garlic and sauté for 1 minute, then add all the spices and stir-fry until you get the aroma of the turmeric.

· Add tomatoes and stir-fry until they are mixed with the onion and spices.

· Cut 5 potatoes into bite-size pieces and add. Mash one potato and set aside. Stir-fry, mixing the potatoes well together for 3 minutes.

Add mashed potato and stir-fry for 1 minute. Add salt.

- Slowly add 2 cups water, stirring the potatoes and seeing that the mashed potatoes do not form into lumps but are dissolved, thickening the curry.

- Cover and simmer for 5 minutes.

- Put eggs in the simmering curry and cook for 7 minutes or so.

- Serve in a shallow dish with potatoes and curry at the bottom and eggs cut lengthwise on top. Sprinkle green coriander on top and serve.

BATATA SOUNG

A Saraswat Brahmin Recipe

Serves 4

500 gm potatoes
1 walnut-sized lump of tamarind
3 tbsp coconut oil
1 tsp mustard seeds
1 sprig curry leaves
4 large onions, finely chopped
1 walnut-sized piece of jaggery
2 tsp chilli powder
1½ tsp coriander powder
Salt to taste

- Boil potatoes in their jackets until cooked. Take care not to overcook. Cut into ¾" cubes and set aside.

- Soak tamarind in 1 cup hot water. Extract juice, discarding pulp.

- Heat oil in a heavy pan, add mustard seeds and curry leaves. When the mustard seeds pop, add onion and sauté until golden brown. Add potato and sauté for 2 to 3 minutes until brown.

- Add tamarind juice, crushed jaggery and all other ingredients. Stir together. Add ¼ cup hot water and salt. Allow water to boil and lower flame.

- On a very low fire simmer for three minutes.

- Serve hot.

MASHED POTATO MASALA

Serves 4

500 gm potatoes
1 tbsp corn oil
1 tsp mustard seeds
1 dry red chilli
1 tsp black gram (urad dal), washed
1 tsp Bengal gram (chana dal), washed
2 medium-sized onions, finely chopped
2 tomatoes, chopped
1" piece ginger, chopped
½ green chilli, chopped
½ tsp turmeric powder
Salt to taste
½ cup green peas, boiled
1 sprig curry leaves

- Boil potatoes in their jackets until cooked soft. Peel and mash coarsely and set aside.

- Heat oil, add all the spices, curry leaves and dals. When mustard seeds pop, add onion, tomato, ginger, green chilli and turmeric. Sauté for 2 minutes.

- Add 1 cup water, salt to taste and mix together. Cover pan and simmer for 3 minutes.

- Add peas and simmer for 3 minutes.

- Finally, add potato and stir the mixture well. If necessary, sprinkle water and cook further till done.

- Serve hot. Can be eaten as a snack or with parantha or chapatti.

p u m p k i n

Large pumpkins kept in a heap in markets are a wonderful sight. Pumpkins are commonly seen growing in small gardens or in tiny spaces carved out in the city by new migrants from villages. They carefully nurture the pumpkin shoots, making a little net of strings to coax the plant to grow. All parts of this precious plant are eaten—the leaves, the stems, the beautiful yellow flowers— and, of course, the golden fruit is preserved for a feast day.

There are a range of pumpkins available. We get here the yellow pumpkin, which we call *kaddu* or *sitaphal*, and the green pumpkin which we call *petha*. The *kaddu* is made into a number of dishes to be eaten during meals while the *petha* is used for making sweets. Some believe that the pumpkin must have come from the Middle East or Asia, for the earliest word in French is *potiron*, a derivative of the Arabic word for morel mushrooms. However, its origins are from the New World, where it was used by the local inhabitants from prehistoric times. Ancient tombs dating to 2000 BC give evidence that pumpkin and squash were used as important food items.

Pumpkins are an unpopular vegetable. My friend, Peter Lawton, is the only person I know who adores the pumpkin and is even willing to eat it raw. He has a Pavlovian response when you mention pumpkin, which I find very amusing. Perhaps it was because he grew up in New Zealand where pumpkins were never cooked but were fed to the pigs. His reaction must have originally been aesthetic. He must have seen those beautifully shaped and coloured pumpkins in heaps in the markets and not being able to taste them must have aroused his appetite for them. The pumpkin is not only a versatile and easy vegetable to cook but abounds in minerals and has a high potassium content. The green pumpkin—*petha*—is an excellent diuretic and is also cooling. It is prescribed by naturopaths and ayurvedics to be taken as a juice for detoxification.

I generally don't like eating pumpkins unless—I hate to sound immodest—they are cooked according to my recipes!

GOLDEN SOUP

Pumpkin Soup

Serves 6

1 kg pumpkin
5 cloves garlic, finely chopped
½ tsp black pepper
½ tsp salt
Juice of 2 limes
2 tbsp chopped basil or mint for cold soup
12 young fresh spinach leaves (optional)

· Clean pumpkin thoroughly. Cut into small pieces with the skin. Remove seeds and fibres.

· Heat 6 cups water in a pan.

· Add garlic, black pepper and salt to taste.

· When the water boils, add pumpkin. Cook for 15 to 20 minutes until soft.

· Mix in blender, adding juice of 2 limes. The soup should have a lemony tang but should not be too sour.

· This soup can be served cold, garnished with basil or mint.

· If it is to be served hot, after the above steps, add spinach leaves to the soup and heat with the lid on before serving. Serve with toasted bread.

This soup is light and delicious. It is excellent for the kidney and for general health and can be easily digested. I hit upon this recipe when I was trying to flush my kidneys. The soups that I make do not have any thickening agent nor are they cooked with any oil. In fact, they are a simple purée of vegetables. They can be made from all types of pumpkins, from green squash to the zucchini family.

GOLDEN SUNRISE

Pumpkin with Sour Plums and Spinach

Serves 6

2 kg pumpkin
100 gm sour dried plums (alu bukhara)
1 golf-ball sized lump of tamarind
2 tbsp mustard oil
2 dry red chillies
1 tsp panch phoron
1 tbsp brown sugar (shakkar)
1 bunch tender spinach leaves
1 tsp salt

- Skin the pumpkin and cut into 1" pieces.

- Wash plums and put in enough hot water to cover.

- Soak tamarind in hot water which is sufficient to cover the shredded pieces.

- Heat oil until it smokes.

- Remove from fire, add red chillies and panch phoron. Return to the fire and add pumpkin.

- Stir until fully coated with oil.

- Add plums along with the water and brown sugar.

- Cover and cook for 10 minutes or until the pumpkin is cooked fully.

- Sieve the tamarind and add only the juice.

- Stir so that everything is mixed well.

- Add spinach leaves on top, cover and set aside.

159

- Reheat before serving.
- Serve in a jade green or white dish, taking care to display all the colours of the ingredients.

This dish combines a sour and sweet taste. It is based on a Shirazi recipe without the meat but with some Indian spices to add to the flavour.

CRUSTY VALLEY

Pumpkin and Greens

Serves 6

2 kg pumpkin or half of a pumpkin
2 tsp dried mango powder (amchur)
1 tsp chilli powder
2 tsp cumin powder
2 tsp coriander powder
2 tsp salt
5 tbsp butter
1 kg spinach
500 gm spring onions
125 gm green coriander
250 gm green fenugreek or 4 tbsp dried fenugreek soaked in water
250 gm dill
4 green chillies (optional)
4 eggs

- Take half of the bottom end of the pumpkin.

- Remove all the seeds and fibre. Score the insides by running a fork from the bottom in a deep circular movement, taking care not to pierce the skin.

- Make a paste of amchur, 1 tsp chilli powder, ½ tsp cumin powder, 1 tsp coriander powder and 1 tsp salt with 2 tbsp butter.

- Rub paste into the pumpkin. Bake in an oven at 250° C for 20 to 25 minutes until the insides are cooked thoroughly.

- Wash and chop all the green leafy vegetables and

green chillies as well as the soaked fenugreek and put into a pot. Add salt and remaining spices.

· Cook covered for 15 minutes. Remove from fire, cool and run through a food processor. Add four eggs and blend together. Check for salt and if necessary add some more spices. To the mixture add 3 tbsp butter.

· Pour mixture into the pumpkin and replace in the oven. Cook for 30 minutes at 250°C. The spinach mixture will rise like a soufflé.

· Transfer to a tray. Slice like a cake with the pumpkin skin and serve.

RED PUMPKIN WITH WHOLE CHICKPEAS

Serves 6

3 tbsp white chickpeas (kabuli chana), soaked in water overnight
2 tbsp oil
2 bay leaves
½ tsp panch phoron
1 pinch asafoetida powder
2-3 dry red chillies
2 potatoes, peeled and diced
500 gm red pumpkin, peeled and diced

For paste:

1 dry red chilli
½ tsp turmeric powder
1½ tbsp cumin powder
1½ tbsp coriander powder
1 tbsp chopped ginger
1 tsp dried mango powder (amchur)
Salt to taste
1 tsp sugar
1 tbsp ghee

Seasoning:

1 tsp garam masala powder

· Soak chickpeas overnight. Drain and cook in pressure cooker with 2 cups water for 20 minutes. Drain water and reserve.

· Heat oil in a kadhai. Add bay leaves, panch phoron, asafoetida and red chillies. Stir-fry. Add the potatoes first and fry for 5 minutes. Then add red pumpkin. Stir-fry until vegetables are well fried.

· Make a paste of chilli, turmeric, cumin, coriander, ginger and amchur with a cup of the reserved water from the chickpeas and pour over the vegetables. Add salt and sugar to taste.

· Add drained chickpeas and simmer gently until vegetables are cooked and there is no gravy in the pan.

· Heat before serving and add ghee.

· Add garam masala and mix.

RED PUMPKIN AND RIDGE GOURD COOKED ON BANANA LEAVES

Serves 6

Banana leaves for cooking
Salt to taste
500 gm ridge gourd (touri), peeled and finely chopped
300 gm red pumpkin
2 onions, very finely chopped
4 green chillies, finely chopped
2½ tbsp black mustard seeds
1 tsp turmeric paste
¼ tsp chilli paste
½ coconut, grated
¼ cup oil

- Take 1 banana leaf and cut it to size for the iron tawa. Double the layer. Change leaf with each frying.

- Add ½ tsp salt to ridge gourd and set aside for a while. Then squeeze out the water.

- Peel and cut pumpkin into juliennes. In a bowl mix together the two vegetables and all the other ingredients including oil.

- Place banana leaves on the tawa over medium heat. Spoon the vegetable mixture onto the banana leaves and cook, increasing heat towards end of cooking time until vegetables are cooked and oil comes to the surface.

- Turn vegetables over once during cooking and smooth over with the back of a spoon.

My friends in Uday Villa outside Calcutta, women who have been abandoned by their families, used to cook this on a small stove as we sat together and discussed our future plans.

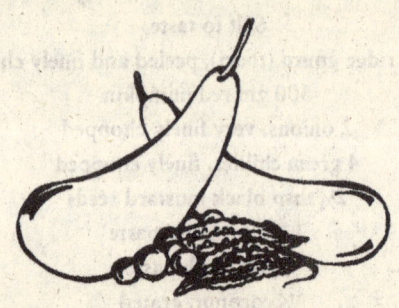

PUMPKIN WITH COCONUT

Serves 6

1 kg red pumpkin
1 tbsp oil
Salt to taste
2 green chillies

For paste:

1 tsp turmeric powder
½ tsp chilli powder
2 tbsp cumin seeds
1 tbsp coriander seeds
½ coconut, grated

For tempering:

1 tbsp ghee or oil
1 pinch asafoetida powder
½ tsp panch phoron
2 bay leaves
2 dry red chillies, broken

· Peel and slice pumpkin into very thin 1" sticks after removing fibre and seeds.

· Heat oil in a kadhai and add pumpkin. Add salt, mix well. Add ¼ cup water, cover and cook for about 5 to 7 minutes over low heat.

· Make a paste of the spices and half the grated coconut. Remove cover from pan. Add paste. Mix well. Continue cooking over medium fire, stirring from time to time. Add the green chillies and continue to cook until nearly all the water evaporates.

- Stir in the remaining grated coconut, mixing well.

- Continue cooking, stirring all the time for another 5 to 7 minutes. Remove from fire.

- In a separate kadhai heat 1 tbsp ghee or oil. Add asafoetida, panch phoron, bay leaves and red chillies. When the panch phoron stops spluttering, add the cooked pumpkin. Mix thoroughly. Cook for two minutes. Remove from fire. Serve with rice or chapatti.

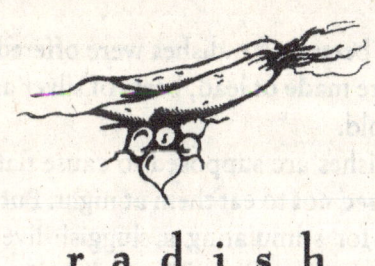

r a d i s h

I always associate the long white radish, smooth and delicious, with winter in Lahore. My mother and cousins would sit basking in the sun with a basketful of fresh radish, straight from the garden. The radishes would be washed and brought to us along with a bowl of salt. We would pull off the outer leaves and keep the tender inner leaves. We would dip the radish in salt placed on our palms and nibble at it. Mother told us to eat the green leaves as well, for it would help our digestion. We used to call them 'repeaters', for our excesses in eating would make us burp. However, radishes were a part of our lives as you can see from the childhood rhyme: *Tarkari lou Tarkari / Malan aiee Bikaner sou / Lai kay tarkari / Mouli ka kila banaya / Gajar ka darwaza / Shakarkandi ki toup banie / Maro farangi raja / Aji dha dhanika / Dhan Dhan Dha.* (From Bikaner your lady gardener has come with vegetables. Of radishes I have made a fort and a gate of carrots. Of sweet potatoes I have made a gun, to kill the foreign Raja. Let's sing and beat the drum. Dha dhanika, dhan dhan dha!)

The radish was known to ancient civilizations. The Egyptians ate it and the workers were given radishes and garlic as a part of their payment for working on the great temples. Pliny in his *Natural History* mentions that in

Delphi turnips, beets and radishes were offered to Apollo. The turnips were made of lead, beets of silver and radishes of burnished gold.

In India radishes are supposed to cause flatulence and people are advised not to eat them at night. But the juice of radish is good for stimulating a sluggish liver and is an important cure for jaundice. The radish has substantial amounts of potassium and calcium while the leaves are very rich in minerals and Vitamins A and C.

These days, the tiny pink radishes are more popular than the large white winter radish.

MOOLI KACHUMBAR

Radish Crushed

Serves 6

3 large white radish, cleaned
3 tbsp lime juice
Salt and pepper to taste

· Remove all the big radish leaves and set aside. Retain fresh inner leaves.

· Grate radish.

· Rub the inner leaves in both hands to tenderize. Then chop them fine.

· Mix all ingredients together.

· Refrigerate for 1 hour before serving.

Keep the leaves for mooli ki sabzi (p.174).

MIXED KACHUMBAR

Serves 6

2 white radish
1 cucumber
1 onion, chopped coarsely
3 large tomatoes, chopped
3 tbsp lime juice
Salt and pepper to taste

- Clean radish, keep aside tender leaves.
- Cut radish into small cubes and chop up young leaves as directed in previous recipe (p.171).
- Peel cucumber, check for bitterness, and cut into cubes.
- Mix all the vegetables together with lime juice, salt and pepper.
- Refrigerate before serving.

RADISH AND ORANGE SALAD

Serves 6

1 bunch small round pink radish
3 oranges
1 tbsp crushed walnuts
½ tsp salt
1 tbsp lime juice

· Wash radish, removing the stems except the tender ones in the middle. Slice them in roundels, keeping the leafy part vertical so that leaves get cut along with the roundels. Place in a bowl.

· Peel oranges and separate segments. Skin segments, remove seeds and add the orange pieces to the salad.

· Sprinkle walnuts, salt and lime juice and toss lightly.

A delicious salad which is also a feast for the eyes, this can be served at the end of a meal or with beer on a leisurely Sunday.

MOOLI KI SABZI

Radish with Leaves Sautéed

Serves 6

3 tbsp oil
2 dry red chillies
3 large white radish with leaves
Radish leaves, approx. 1 kg
1 tsp bishop's weed (ajwain)
1 tsp salt

- Heat oil in a kadhai. Add dry chillies and remove from fire.

- Cut radish into thin roundels and chop leaves fine.

- Replace kadhai on fire, add chopped radish and fry.

- Add leaves, ajwain and salt and sauté for 8 to 10 minutes until crisp.

- This is delicious with chapatti or parantha. But don't forget—only for lunch.

We throw away the most nutritious part of vegetables—their leaves. Retain the leaves of radish for making this *sabzi*.

MOOLI KI ROTI

Radish Chapatti

Serves 6

500 gm wholewheat flour
1 tsp salt
½ tsp bishop's weed (ajwain)
1 kg white radish, grated
1 tsp dried pomegranate seeds
½ tsp chilli powder

· Add ½ tsp salt and the ajwain to flour and mix together. Knead into dough and keep covered with a napkin for 1 hour.

· Grate radish and squeeze out extra water.

· Pound the pomegranate seeds into fine particles and add along with all the remaining ingredients to the grated radish. Mix.

· Roll out a thin chapatti 6" in diameter, place 2 tbsp of the radish mix and spread on the chapatti, leaving ½" at the edges. Place another chapatti on top and press down all around firmly. Gently press down with the palm of your hand.

· Lift and transfer to a hot griddle or tawa. After half a minute, when the chapatti is semi-cooked, with a folded napkin rotate the chapatti for half a minute.

· Using a wide spatula turn the chapatti over and repeat the process.

· Now press down firmly with the napkin and cook on

both sides until brown spots appear on the surface. Remove and set aside.

· Butter may be served on the side. Traditionally, a parantha is fried in ghee or oil. I generally avoid doing that. However, there is a way to make the fried parantha with less ghee. After the roti has been cooked and brown spots appear, take ½ tsp oil or ghee and rub it on the top and turn over. Rotate it so that the griddle gets coated with oil, then turn down the flame. Add ½ tsp oil to the other side and repeat the process.

· Serve straight from the griddle with curd and mint chutney.

CURRIED RADISH

Serves 6

4 fresh, large white radish, diced
2 tbsp oil
2 large potatoes, diced
100 gm green peas, shelled
1 dry red chilli
½ tsp cumin seeds
Salt and sugar to taste

For paste:

2 dry red chillies, broken
1 pinch cumin seeds
½ tsp turmeric powder

For tempering:

1 dry red chilli
1½ tbsp aniseed
1 tsp ghee
1 dry red chilli
1 tsp garam masala powder

· Parboil radish. Drain and squeeze out water. Set aside.

· Heat 1 tbsp oil in a kadhai and lightly brown potatoes.

· Heat remaining oil in another kadhai, add chilli and cumin seeds and stir-fry for half a minute. Add radish, stir and add paste made of chillies, cumin and turmeric. Add salt and sugar. Cover and cook for 5 minutes. Add the potatoes and peas. Add ½ cup water. Stir and simmer until all the vegetables are done.

· Heat 1 tsp ghee, fry chilli and aniseed. Stir in garam masala and saute for a few minutes, add to the vegetable and mix together.

177

Singhara

Singhara, or water chestnut, is an indigenous vegetable and is mentioned in the Vedic texts. It is treated as a ritually pure food and is eaten during religious ceremonies, period of fasting, as well as by sanyasis. During the *navaratra* fasts when *anna*, staple food such as wheat flour and rice, is not permitted, flour made from dried water chestnuts is used.

It is grown in tanks and is eaten fresh as a fruit, and is also boiled and eaten. Ancient literature mentions different dishes made with it. Nowadays, only the flour is cooked during the period of fasting.

SINGHARAVA ANAR

Water Chestnut and Pomegranate Salad

Serves 6

1 kg fresh water chestnuts (singhara)
1 large cucumber
2 spring onions
1 pomegranate
⅓ tsp salt
¼ tsp black pepper
2 tbsp vinegar

- Soak water chestnuts in water and wash thoroughly.

- Peel the skin and inner creamish layer until the white kernel appears. Chop lengthwise and put in a serving bowl.

- Peel cucumber, check that it is not bitter, chop into small bite-size pieces, add to the bowl.

- Wash spring onions thoroughly before cutting. Chop fine and add to the bowl.

- Crack the pomegranate, take out the seeds and add.

- Now put in salt. pepper and vinegar. Toss together and serve.

SINGHARA AND SEM SALAD

Water Chestnut and Green Broad Beans Salad

Serves 6

1 kg water chestnuts (singhara)
1 kg green broad beans (sem)
1 tbsp white sesame seeds, roasted
1 tsp salt
⅓ tsp black pepper
2 tbsp oil
2 tbsp vinegar

- Soak singhara in water and wash thoroughly. Peel the skin and inner creamish layer until the white kernel appears. Chop lengthwise and put in a serving bowl.

- Wash and string sem and chop into 1" pieces. Put water to boil, add ⅓ tsp salt. Add sem in boiling water, allow it to come to a boil. Cook for 2 minutes, drain water thoroughly and add to the bowl.

- Mix three-quarters of the sesame seeds, the salt, pepper, oil and vinegar and toss together. Sprinkle remaining sesame on top and serve.

SINGHARA, HARA DHANIA AND KALA CHANA SALAD

Water Chestnut, Green Coriander and Black Chickpea Salad

Serves 6

1 cup black chickpeas (kala chana), soaked overnight
2 onions
6 cloves garlic
1 tsp salt
500 gm water chestnuts (singhara)
100 gm green coriander
1 tbsp olive oil or corn oil
3 tbsp vinegar
¼ tsp chilli powder

· Cook black chickpeas in water with 1 onion, garlic and ½ tsp salt in pressure cooker for 20 minutes. Check if done, otherwise cook under pressure for extra 5 minutes. Drain and keep liquid for soups.

· Soak water chestnuts and wash thoroughly. Peel and remove inner creamish skin. Chop lengthwise and put in bowl.

· Wash and chop coriander leaves with stems and add to *singhara*.

· Chop 1 onion fine and add.

· See that the black chickpeas are fully drained, then add to the bowl. Now add salt, chilli powder, oil and vinegar and toss vigorously. Set aside for half an hour and then refrigerate or serve directly.

SINGHARA AND MOONG DAL SALAD

Water Chestnut and Lentil Salad

Serves 6

1 cup green gram (moong dal), hulled, washed and soaked overnight
500 gm water chestnuts (singhara)
100 gm spring onions, washed and finely chopped
50 gm green coriander or mint
2 green chillies
½ tsp salt
¼ tsp black pepper
1 tbsp corn oil
1 tbsp vinegar

- Drain moong dal thoroughly and put in a serving bowl.

- Soak, wash and peel water chestnuts. Chop water chestnuts lengthwise and add to dal.

- Add onion to bowl.

- Wash clean and chop coriander or mint and add.

- Mix all the other ingredients, pour into the bowl and mix well. Serve directly or refrigerate.

HARI PIAZ AUR SINGHARA KI SABZI

Spring Onions and Water Chestnuts Sauteed

Serves 4

2 tbsp corn oil
2 dry red chillies
1 tsp panch phoron
1 kg spring onions, washed and chopped
500 gm singhara, washed, peeled and chopped lengthwise
1 tbsp vinegar
½ tsp salt

· Heat oil in wok, add dry chillies and *panch phoron*, stir for half a minute.

· As it pops, add spring onions and stir over a high flame for 2 minutes.

· Add *singharas* and stir-fry for half a minute. Mix in vinegar and salt. Remove from fire and serve immediately.

TAMATAR AUR SINGHARA KI SABZI

Tomatoes and Water Chestnuts Sautéed

Serves 4

2 tbsp corn oil
⅛ tsp asafoetida powder
2 dry red chillies
1 tsp panch phoron
3 onions, cut lengthwise
750 gm tomatoes, each cut lengthwise into 6 to 8 pieces
500 gm singhara, washed, peeled and chopped lengthwise
2 tbsp raisins, washed and soaked in water for 1 hour
1 tsp salt
2 tbsp vinegar
1 tbsp brown sugar (shakkar)

- Heat oil in wok, add asafoetida, dry chillies and panch phoron. When it pops, add onion and fry until transparent.

- Add tomatoes and stir gently for 1 minute.

- Add singhara and stir-fry for half a minute.

- Drain raisins, add to the wok.

- Mix salt, vinegar and brown sugar and pour into the wok. Mix gently. Cover and cook for a minute.

- Serve directly.

s p i n a c h a n d
o t h e r g r e e n s

Fresh green spinach is a versatile vegetable that originated in Persia and can be prepared in a number of ways. In Iran, green herbs form an important part of urban and village life. In the cities, fresh green herbs—*sabzi khordan*—are a part of every meal. They are eaten raw with paneer, *murabba* and nuts for breakfast and with lunch and dinner. Iranians have a great love for greens and one of their most delicious dishes is *kukeh sarah*, a kind of quiche made from herbs collected from the mountainside in early spring. As the snow melts, the sides of the mountains start becoming green with herbs, which spring up as though in front of your eyes. Women and children begin collecting them. With great care they separate the herbs which can be eaten raw and those which can be cooked. Nouroz, the Persian New Year feast, has a *sabzi pulao* made from herbs and fried fish as essential items on the menu.

Herbs have been part of the Persian tradition since time immemorial and the royal gardeners must have cultivated these herbs. Spinach was one of them and according to literary references the seeds were carried far and wide, even into the remote Himalayan kingdoms. The Persian word, *aspanak,* or spinach, came to Europe via the Arab world. The great Tang Emperor, Tai Tsung, was sent the spinach plant in the seventh century as a tribute. The Emperor celebrated his first taste of spinach in verse and even had it mentioned in the chronicles. Perhaps the simple, delicious way in which spinach is still served in Chinese cuisine may be a continuation of that tradition, as my dear friend Ranbir Vohra told us. Ranbir, who is a Sinologist, is also a great gourmet and his wife Meena is a wonderful cook. Eating a Chinese meal with them was always an experience as Ranbir would regale us with the history of each dish.

SPINACH SOUP

Serves 6

1 kg fresh spinach
5 cloves garlic, finely chopped
1 large onion, coarsely chopped
1 tbsp grated ginger
Salt to taste
1 cup curd, beaten smooth
½ tsp black pepper or paprika

· Wash spinach thoroughly.

· Chop with stems and put in a pan on the fire.

· Add garlic, onion, ginger and salt to taste.

· Add 2 cups water and cook for 10 minutes. Cool and run through blender.

· Add 4 cups water and cook for 5 minutes more before serving. Taste for salt.

· To serve it cold, refrigerate overnight or for a minimum of 4 hours.

· Remove from refrigerator and mix well together.

· Serve with a dollop of low-fat curd, sprinkled with pepper.

· When serving it hot, serve in a large tureen with beaten curd by the side and chilli powder or paprika in a small bowl.

SPINACH AND CURD COLD SOUP

Serves 6

- For a spinach and curd cold soup follow the recipe for Spinach Soup (p.187), only reduce the spinach to 500 gm and put in 1 cup water while cooking.

- Mix the cooked spinach with 2 cups low-fat curd in a blender, add 1 cup cold water and chill.

- Serve with a sprinkling of freshly roasted, finely-powdered cumin.

- This soup should not be had by those who have kidney problems. It's very good for anaemia and is a must, once a week, for those suffering from it.

PAALAK KADHI SHORBA

Thickened Spinach and Curd Soup

Serves 6

500 gm spinach
½ cup chickpea flour (besan)
1 tsp salt
½ tsp turmeric powder
¼ tsp chilli powder
3 cups curd
2 dry red chillies
1 tsp brown mustard seeds
1 tsp cumin seeds
10 curry leaves
1" piece ginger, grated
1 tbsp black cumin seeds

- Clean and wash the spinach thoroughly. Remove the stems and discard. Chop the leaves fine and set aside.

- Mix besan with salt, turmeric and chilli powders. Add 3 cups curd and mix into a smooth paste.

- Slowly add 4 cups water, mixing together so as not to leave any lumps.

- Heat 1 tbsp oil in a pan, add dry red chillies, mustard seeds, cumin seeds, curry leaves, ginger, and sauté briskly.

- When the mustard starts to pop, add the spinach and sauté. Now add curd mixture. Stir together, mixing all the ingredients. Lower fire and cook for 10 minutes until the mixture thickens. Continue to stir.

189

- If too thick, add hot water to thin. Cook for a further 5 minutes after adding water. Taste the sauce to ensure that the smell and taste of the *besan* has been absorbed. Set aside.

- Remove from fire.

- Roast 1 tbsp whole black cumin. Pound it in a mortar and sprinkle on soup. Serve hot.

This can be eaten as a soup with Lebanese bread soaked in it—a meal in itself—or with a bowl of plain, steamed rice. It is delicious if served with roasted papad and dry cooked vegetables.

KHATTE WALA SAAG

Sour Greens' Soup

Serves 6

½ cup rice flour
½ tsp turmeric powder
1 tsp salt
¼ tsp chilli powder
2 cups curd
1 tsp oil
1 dry red chilli
1 pinch asafoetida powder
500 gm amaranth (chulie) or spinach
1" ginger, grated

· Mix turmeric, salt and chilli powder to the rice flour.

· Add 1 cup curd to the above and make into a smooth paste. Mix the remaining curd, taking care that no lumps are formed. Add 4 cups water and set aside.

· Heat oil in a kadhai. When it begins to smoke, add dry red chilli and asafoetida.

· Add chopped greens, grated ginger and sauté briskly for 1 minute.

· Add ¼ cup water, cover with a lid and simmer for 2 minutes on a low fire.

· Slowly add curd mixture, stirring all the while, and let it simmer.

· Continue to stir until the mixture thickens. Cook for 10 minutes on a low fire.

Serve hot.

This is a delicious hot soup that can also be eaten with rice or chapatti. These are recipes from my childhood which was spent in the mountains of NWFP in Zilla Hazara where vegetables were not available during winter and the choice was limited even in summer. Buttermilk, however, was available in plenty and was even given away to neighbours. These recipes were made with buttermilk and dried leaves in winter. This simple, inexpensive fare was meant only for the family and was never served to a visitor.

PAALAK AUR DAHI

Spinach with Curd

Serves 6

2 tbsp butter
6 cloves garlic, crushed
2 tsp cumin powder
½ tsp chilli powder
1 tsp salt
1 kg spinach, cleaned and kept whole with tender stems
1 cup curd, beaten smooth

- Put 1 tbsp butter in kadhai and sauté half the garlic for half a minute. Add 1 tsp cumin, chilli powder and salt. Sauté for half a minute.

- Add spinach and sauté, turning briskly until the spices and spinach are mixed well. Continue to stir for 2 minutes.

- Sprinkle water generously, lower flame, cover and simmer for 5 minutes. Remove from fire.

- Lift spinach from the pot and place on a shallow serving dish. Pour curd over the spinach.

- Heat 1 tsp butter in a small frying pan. Add 1 tsp cumin powder and stir for half a minute, add remaining garlic and sauté till golden.

- Pour over spinach and curd and serve.

- Ideally, this dish should be prepared just before serving.

SPINACH À LA KOKOKA

Serves 6

1 kg fresh small-leaved spinach
1½ tsp salt
2 tsp light soya sauce
1 tsp sesame oil
½ tsp black pepper
2 tbsp oil

- Wash spinach in plenty of water, keeping the young stems intact. Stack leaves evenly on a long, thin towel.

- Put a large pot of water on the fire, add salt. When the water boils, lower the leaves with the towel into the water. Boil for 2 minutes and lift out of pot and put in a large colander, gently removing the towel. Allow to drain.

- Mix salt, soya sauce, sesame oil and pepper. Arrange the leaves on a plate and pour the mixture over them.

- Serve hot or at room temperature.

This is based on a Shinto recipe.

SAUTÉD SPINACH

Serves 6

2 kg spinach
1 tsp salt
½ tsp black pepper
1 tbsp malt vinegar
1 tbsp sesame oil
2 dry red chillies

- Wash spinach, keep fresh young stems and discard the thick ones.

- Mix salt and pepper with ½ tbsp vinegar and set aside.

- Put kadhai with oil on a high flame.

- Add red chillies and sauté for half a minute.

- Add spinach and sauté briskly.

- Add the remaining vinegar while sautéing. Sprinkle salt and pepper.

- Remove from fire and transfer spinach to a serving dish.

- Pour the sauce on top of the spinach and serve hot.

CRISP SPINACH

Serves 6

2 kg spinach
3 tbsp sesame oil
1 tsp rock salt
½ tsp black pepper

- Wash spinach thoroughly, discard thick stems.

- Wrap in soft towel and dry thoroughly.

- Chop spinach into fine strips.

- Put kadhai with oil on a high flame.

- Add spinach, salt and pepper and sauté, stirring constantly, until crisp.

- Serve as a starter or as a side dish with noodles or *khichri*.

CHAMAN MAI NARGIS

Narcissus in the Meadow

Serves 4

3 tbsp butter
2 onions, coarsely chopped
6 cloves garlic, finely chopped
1 kg spinach, cleaned and chopped with the stems
250 gm spring onions, finely chopped with leaves
1 tsp salt
100 gm green coriander, chopped with the stems
2 tbsp cornflour
½ tsp chilli powder (optional)
4 eggs

- Melt 2 tbsp butter in a kadhai. Add onion and garlic and sauté until lightly browned.

- Add spinach and spring onion and toss briskly, mixing them together. Stir-fry for 2 minutes.

- Sprinkle salt and cover. Lower the flame and allow spinach to simmer for 5 minutes.

- Add coriander and mix together.

- Purée in a liquidizer.

- On a dry griddle roast the cornflour by stirring until it begins to get slightly brown.

- Put the puréed spinach and greens in the pan, add the roasted flour and stir well.

- Correct seasoning. If you like your food hot, add ½

tsp chilli powder and mix.

· Cook the puréed spinach for 5 minutes.

· Lightly butter a 9" round baking dish. Pour in the spinach mix, smoothing the top carefully.

· Cook in oven at 200°C for 5 to 7 minutes until it starts to set. Remove from oven.

· Crack open 4 eggs and pour out half the egg white, leaving the rest in the shell.

· Make four round 1" holes in the set spinach and pour in the eggs (yolks with half the egg whites). Return to the oven and bake for 20 minutes. Serve hot.

The yellow of the egg, surrounded by a white halo on a green base, looks like narcissus peeping out from a green herbaceous garden. This is a dish that I learnt from my Shirazi friend, Feranghiz Shadman.

KHORESTH SPINACH VA ALBALU

Spinach, Chickpea and Dried Sour Plums

Serves 6

2 kg spinach, washed, thick stems removed, and chopped
2 tbsp corn oil
2 dry red chillies
1 stick cinnamon
2 bay leaves
6 green cardamoms, crushed
2 onions, finely chopped
6 cloves garlic, finely chopped
2 cups chickpeas, boiled
1½ tsp salt
½ tsp chilli powder
250 gm dried sour plums, soaked overnight

- Wash spinach. Remove thick stems and chop coarsely.

- Heat oil in a pan. Add dry chillies, cinnamon, bay leaves and cardamom and sauté for half a minute.

- Add onions and garlic and sauté. When browned, add chickpeas, salt and chilli powder and sauté for 2 minutes.

- Now add spinach, sour plums, and water as required and stir together. Cook uncovered for 10 minutes.

- Serve with rice or by itself.

KUKEH ESPINACH

Spinach Soufflé

Serves 6

3 tbsp oil
2 kg spinach, washed and chopped with stems
500 gm spring onions, washed and chopped with leaves
2 green chillies, finely chopped
1 tsp salt
4 eggs
2 tbsp cornflour
6 cloves garlic

- Heat oil in a pan and add spinach, onion, green chillies, salt and turn swiftly till all the leaves are covered with oil. Stir-fry for 5 minutes.

- Sprinkle water and cover. Simmer on low fire for 5 minutes.

- Cool and purée in the liquidizer, along with 4 eggs, cornflour and garlic, and mix well.

- Butter a deep dish and put in the mixture.

- Bake in an oven at 250°C for 20 minutes till it rises. Serve immediately.

- This dish can be served with curd and can also be eaten cold. A favourite Iranian dish.

Vegetables

KUKEH SABZI SARRAH

Herb Soufflé

I love this herb soufflé which is similar to the spinach one but is basically made from herbs collected from the sides of the mountains. This harks back to the pastoral days in Iran when the cold winter deprived people of green vegetables. As the snow melted, women and children all over the country fanned out on the mountainside to gather edible herbs.

I make this soufflé with whatever herbs are available, but with a balance of flavours. With spinach as the base you can put in a small bunch of fenugreek leaves, coriander leaves and stems, 100 gm amaranth leaves, 2 bunches of mint and spring onions. It can be made exactly in the same way as Spinach Soufflé (p. 200).

tomato

Tomatoes are a part of our daily food. They can be eaten as a salad, as part of a sauce or even to give flavour and colour to our curries. One cannot imagine what the cooks did until eighteenth century AD when tomatoes were introduced by the English to India. They originally came from Latin America and have been used in Peru and Mexico since pre-historic times. It was in the sixteenth century that Spanish explorers introduced it to Europe. The name comes from the Mexican word tomatl. We call it *tamatar* or *vilayati baingan*, European aubergine. Anyway, the tomatoes we find in India are delicious and not like the tasteless ones you get in England or USA. What is horrifying is that in America they are trying to grow tomatoes which are in the form of cubes. All this to ease transportation, who cares if they don't taste like tomatoes!

The luscious red tomatoes were known in Europe as love apples. Perhaps that is why in England they had the reputation of arousing excessive sexual appetites, and people were advised to eat them in moderation.

Today, tomatoes are an important part of most cuisines in Europe and the Middle East. They are also known as 'protective foods' because of their nutritive value and are rich in Vitamins A and C as well as high on potassium and sodium. Recent research in Europe has indicated that the low rate of heart disease amongst Italians is because of their high intake of small cherry tomatoes, red leaved bitterish salad and, of course, red wine. However, those suffering from kidney problems are advised not to eat tomatoes.

TOMATO AND ORANGE SOUP

Serves 6

500 gm ripe tomatoes, skinned and chopped
2 onions, finely chopped
2 fresh carrots, chopped
1½ tsp salt
2 tsp sugar
1 tsp black pepper
8 large oranges or 2 cups orange juice and 2 oranges peeled
1 lime
1 tbsp chopped basil

- Add tomato, onion and carrot to 4 cups boiling water. Cook with salt, sugar and pepper until carrots are tender.

- Cool and purée.

- Extract the juice of 6 oranges and the lime and add to the soup.

- Separate the remaining oranges, peel each segment, remove seeds, and lightly scatter on top of the soup.

- Sprinkle basil and serve warm. Can also be served cold.

If oranges are not available, add 2 cups orange juice, but select the juice which is the closest in taste to fresh juice.

TOMATO AND EGG SALAD

Serves 6

8 eggs
10 medium-sized tomatoes
1 onion, finely chopped
¾ cup vinaigrette dressing made preferably with olive oil

- Boil eggs for 15 minutes and peel.
- While the eggs are boiling, quarter the tomatoes and mix with onion.
- Cut eggs lengthwise into four pieces while hot and put in with the tomatoes.
- Add dressing and toss together.
- Serve at room temperature.

This is an Italian salad that I learnt from my Italian friend Sylvana who would make this instant salad whenever unexpected guests dropped in. She would boil the eggs on one burner, prepare pasta on the other and serve the guests a quick lunch. It reminded me of the *ande ki bhujjia* (scrambled savoury eggs) which was quickly put together at home if people dropped in at mealtime unexpectedly.

TOMATO SALAD WITH CREAM CHEESE SAUCE

Serves 6

1 kg tomatoes
Salt and pepper to taste
1 large onion, finely chopped
1 cup home-made cottage cheese (paneer)
½ cup vinaigrette sauce

- Blanch tomatoes and skin.

- Cut tomatoes in roundels.

- Sprinkle salt and pepper.

- Add onion and mix in paneer. Add vinaigrette and toss well, but lightly. Refrigerate and then serve.

GRILLED TOMATOES

Serves 6

6 medium-sized tomatoes
1½ tsp salt
½ tsp black pepper
2 tsp dried mint, stems removed and crushed
1 tsp sugar
1 tbsp vinegar
2 tsp olive oil

- Slice the bottom of tomatoes and discard. Butter baking dish and place tomatoes stem side down.

- Sprinkle a pinch of salt and pepper over each tomato and plenty of mint.

- Mix salt, pepper, sugar, vinegar and oil in ¾ cup water. Dribble some with spoon on to tomatoes. Pour the rest into the dish from the side.

- Bake in oven at 250°C for half an hour.

- Serve immediately.

Goes very well with pasta or noodles.

mixed
vegetables

Sometimes a combination of vegetables makes far more interesting and stimulating fare than a dish made out of a single vegetable. This category of recipes is particularly useful when one has to deal with leftover vegetables in the refrigerator or from the previous day's meal. Mixed vegetable dishes are also more appealing to the eye and to the palate, combining as they do a variety of textures, colours and flavours.

SAB RANG RASA

Mixed Vegetable Delight

Serves 6

500 gm bottle gourd
2 medium-sized zucchini
2 long aubergines
1 snake gourd
2 green bananas
2 potatoes
100 gm green broad beans (sem)
4 tbsp corn oil
2 dry red chillies
1 tsp mustard seeds
10 curry leaves
1½ tsp salt
½ tsp turmeric powder
½ coconut, grated
1 cup curd

For tempering:

2 tbsp butter
1 tsp cumin seeds

· Cut bottle gourd as for pickle (p.52). Cut ½" thick roundels of zucchini, aubergine and snake gourd. Cut 1" thick roundels of bananas with the skin. Slice potatoes with skin. String and chop sem.

· Heat 3 tbsp oil in a kadhai. Add red chillies and mustard seeds. When mustard seeds begin to pop, add all the vegetables, curry leaves, salt and turmeric. Mix the vegetables, so that they are coated with the oil. Continue to stir for 2 minutes.

· Add 1 cup water. Cover and allow to come to a boil. Immediately lower heat and simmer for 15 minutes.

· Add the grated coconut and mix together.

· Remove from fire.

· Before serving, heat the vegetable and remove from fire. Beat curd and add to the vegetables.

· In a small pan heat melt butter. Add cumin and stir-fry until brown. Pour on the vegetable mix and serve.

The vegetables should be served hot. When serving see that everyone gets a medley of all the vegetables.

MIXED VEGETABLE ENERGY SOUP FOR DETOXIFICATION

Serves 6

500 gm carrots, chopped
500 gm bottle gourd, cleaned and chopped with skin
2 capsicums, deseeded and chopped
500 gm cucumber, peeled, checked for bitterness and cut
500 gm tomatoes, skinned
2 green chillies, finely chopped
10 cloves garlic
2 large onions
3 tbsp lime juice
1 kg cabbage, finely cut

· Put all the ingredients except cabbage and lime juice in a large pan, cover with water and boil for 5 minutes.

· Remove from fire. Cool and run through liquidizer.

· Add lime juice.

· Add cabbage and reheat.

This soup is meant actually for one person to consume during the day. You should have it in the morning and it should be your main food throughout the day. Whenever you feel hungry, have a large bowl of soup. Drink it in a cup as you might drink tea, in a glass as a drink, in a bowl for lunch and dinner. If you feel like eating something solid, make a salad of chopped cabbage, cucumber and onion with lime juice.

Take it for 2 to 3 days without carbohydrates i.e. potatoes, rice or flour, without salt, sugar, oil and alcohol and aerated drinks. You will not feel hungry, rather you will feel energized. This soup is ideal for times when you feel lethargic and bloated or when you have overindulged in food and drink.

MIXED VEGETABLES WITH DIP

Serves 6 to 8

1 small cauliflower, separated into florets
2 carrots, cut into long sticks
1 celery heart, cut into sticks

· Serve on a platter with a dip made from yoghurt or curd blended with mint chutney or salt, red chilli powder and ground roasted sesame.

· You can improvise your own dip. See p. 331-342 for more recipes.

CHENCHRA

Vegetable Peels Sautéed

Serves 6

2 tbsp oil
2 dry red chillies
¼ tsp mustard seeds
½ tsp turmeric powder
2 cups peels from bottle gourd, pumpkin and potatoes,
washed thoroughly and cut in fine juliennes
1 onion, finely sliced

- Heat oil in a pan. Add dry chillies, mustard seeds and turmeric powder. Cook until it stops spluttering.

- Add julienned peel and the onion. Continue frying until onion becomes soft and the peel is cooked. If too dry while cooking, sprinkle water as and when necessary.

- Serve with rice.

A delicious Bengali speciality in which nothing is wasted. This recipe uses peels, the most nutritious part of a vegetable.

A Bengali gourmet friend, Ruby Pal Choudary, was thrilled to see this recipe in the book. According to her it has not featured in any cookery book so far.

A LIGHTLY SPICED
VEGETABLE STEW

Serves 6-8

1 tbsp mustard oil
2 cups stems and very young leaves of the marrow of pumpkin plant,
cut in 1½" or 2" long pieces
2 medium-sized potatoes, cubed
1 brinjal, cut lengthwise
1 radish, cut in roundels
1 green banana, cut in roundels with peel
8-10 green chillies, slit

For paste:
¼ tsp turmeric powder
1" ginger, finely grated
2 tsp coriander seeds

For tempering:
1 tsp ghee
¼ tsp onion seeds
1 tsp cumin seeds, coarsely ground
2 green chillies, coarsely ground
½ tsp cornflour
2 tbsp milk
Salt and sugar to taste

· Heat mustard oil in a kadhai. Lightly fry the stems
  and leaves of the pumpkin with the vegetables. Cover
  and cook for 5 minutes. Do not overcook.

· Make a paste of turmeric, ginger and coriander and
  add salt. Add paste to the vegetables and stir-fry for
  several minutes gently, permitting the vegetables to
  cook in the water released by them.

- Add the slit green chillies. Add a little more water if necessary and simmer vegetables till done. Remove from fire while there is still quite a lot of light gravy in pan.

- In a separate kadhai or pan, heat one tbsp ghee. Add onion seeds and stir-fry till they stop spluttering. Add cooked vegetables and gravy and bring to a boil. Simmer for 5 minutes.

- Stir in the coarsely ground cumin seeds and green chillies. Simmer for 5 minutes.

- Mix the cornflour and milk together and pour over vegetables. Add salt. Stir and simmer for 5 minutes. Remove from fire.

The important part in cooking this dish is to ensure that the vegetables cook through but do not disintegrate. If they become a mishmash, they will neither look good nor taste good.

SHUKTO

Dry Mixed Vegetable

Serves 6

2 tbsp mustard oil
2 bitter gourd (karela), cut in roundels
2 medium-sized potatoes, cut into ½" pieces
1 brinjal, cut into ½" pieces
1 radish, cut in roundels
1 green banana, cut in roundels
4 parmal, cut lengthwise and then halved
3 drumsticks, cut into 2" long pieces
Salt to taste
½ tsp sugar

For paste:

¼ tsp turmeric powder
1 tsp finely grated ginger
1 tbsp cumin seeds
1 tsp mustard seeds
2 dry red chillies

For tempering:

1 tbsp ghee
½ tsp panch phoron

· Heat oil in a kadhai.

· Stir-fry bitter gourd.

· Add the rest of the vegetables and fry for a few minutes until lightly browned.

· Make a paste of all the spices and mix thoroughly with vegetables.

- Add salt, sugar and mix. Finally add 2 cups water. Continue simmering until vegetables are cooked and the water has evaporated.

- Heat ghee and add panch phoron. Fry till spluttering stops and pour over the simmering vegetables. Mix thoroughly. Simmer for five minutes and remove from fire.

Shukto is a Bengali dish of mixed vegetables and one begins the afternoon meal with it. The bitter taste works up the appetite. It is also ideal for digestion when the weather is hot and humid.

MIXED VEGETABLE PACHADI / SALAD

Serves 4

3 tbsp coconut oil
1 onion, finely chopped
½" piece ginger, finely chopped
1 carrot, diced and boiled
1 cup peas, boiled
1 green chilli, finely chopped
Salt to taste
2 cups curd

For tempering:

1 tsp brown mustard seeds
½ tsp cumin seeds
1 dry red chilli, broken
1 sprig curry leaves

· Heat 2 tbsp oil in a kadhai, add onion, fry till transparent, add ginger and sauté for half a minute.

· Mix all the vegetables, add salt and sauté for 3 minutes. Remove from fire.

· Beat curd till smooth and add to the vegetables.

· In a kadhai heat remaining oil and add all the tempering spices. When the mustard seeds pop, add to curd and mix well together.

AVIAL

Mixed Vegetable Stew

Serves 6

1 yam, peeled and chopped into ½" pieces
2 drumsticks, cleaned and cut into 2" long pieces
1 long brinjal, cut in ½" roundels
1 green banana, peeled and cut in ½" roundels
200 gm ash gourd, peeled and cut into ½" pieces
100 gm snake gourd, cut in ½" roundels
100 gm green broad beans (sem)
1 cup curd
Salt to taste
3 tbsp coconut oil or corn oil
1 sprig curry leaves

For paste:

½ coconut, grated
2 green chillies
1 tsp cumin seeds

- Put yam and drumsticks in 2 cups water and cook for 8 to 10 minutes. Add the rest of the vegetables and cook for 10 minutes or until they are cooked but not mushy.

- While this is cooking, prepare the paste in a blender and add curd. Take the cooked vegetables off the fire and mix in paste gently so as not to crush them.

- Return to the fire only when ready to serve. Stir while heating. Do not allow the stew to boil. Add salt, coconut oil and curry leaves and remove from heat.

some special recipes

Special occasions call for distinctive recipes, and here are some that I have tried and enjoyed.

ASHE TOURSH

Divine Sweet and Sour Soup

Serves 6

3 sticks cinnamon
6 cardamoms
¼ cup sugar
1 tsp salt
1 tsp black pepper
1 cup sour dried plums
½ cup rice
1 cup dried apricots, without seeds
¼ cup chopped walnuts
1 cup chopped green coriander
1 cup white chickpeas (kabuli chana), boiled
⅓ cup lime juice
1 tbsp dried mint (optional)

Boil 6 cups water.

Add cinnamon, cardamoms, sugar, salt, pepper, dried plums and rice and cook for 15 minutes.

Add apricots, walnuts, ⅔ cup coriander and cook for 10 minutes.

· When the water begins to boil, add chickpeas.

· Cover and cook for 15 minutes.

· Add lime juice.

· Heat the soup before serving and add the remaining chopped coriander.

· If green coriander is not available, rub dried mint in

your hand to crush it fine and add it to the soup.

This soup is a great Persian delicacy which is best eaten in summer as it is supposed to have a cooling effect. It can also be eaten cold.

ORANGE SOUP

Serves 6

2 tsp arrowroot
2 vegetable bouillon cubes
2 tbsp sugar
1½ tsp salt
4 cups fresh orange juice
2 tbsp lime juice
150 gm green coriander
1 orange, peeled, separated into segments and skinned

- Mix arrowroot in 2 cups cold water and heat with soup cubes, sugar and salt. Cook until it thickens. Take off the fire.

- Slowly add orange juice, beating it in until the mixture becomes smooth. If necessary, run through a liquidizer so that it is smooth and without any lumps. Add chopped coriander, keeping aside 2 tbsp, and cook on slow fire before serving. Do not allow it to boil.

- Sprinkle orange segments and coriander on top and serve.

This is a delicious soup which has a beautiful orange colour with flecks of green. It is sweet, salty and tangy and creates an appetite for the dishes to follow. It is a soup I developed when a friend sent me a large basket of oranges from Nagpur. I made marmalade, drank fresh juice, offered oranges to the neighbours and tried out this soup.

FRESH MUSHROOMS IN CREAM SAUCE

Serves 6

2 tbsp oil
1 large onion, finely sliced
2 cups sliced mushrooms
½ tsp garlic, minced
2 vegetable bouillon cubes
Salt to taste
4 tbsp cream
2 tbsp cornflour

- Heat 1 tbsp oil in a pan, add onion and mushrooms, sauté until mushrooms soften and release their juice.

- Remove mushrooms and reserve the juice.

- Replace pan on fire, add the remaining oil and garlic, stir, then add mushroom juice.

- Dissolve bouillon in a little water, blend in cornflour and add to the sauce.

- Add cream and salt along with mushrooms.

- Warm on low flame.

FRESH MUSHROOMS

Serves 4

1 tsp butter
1 dry red chilli
6 cloves garlic, finely chopped
200 gm button mushrooms
¼ tsp salt
2 tbsp soya sauce
2 tbsp vinegar
⅛ tsp chilli powder

- Put pan on fire, add butter and dry red chilli. When the butter melts, add garlic and sauté for half a minute.

- Add mushrooms and saute rapidly for a minute or two.

- Add the rest of the ingredients, mixing them together. Cook covered for 5 minutes and take off the fire.

- Serve at room temperature.

SEMI-COOKED SALAD

Serves 6

1 cup florets of broccoli
1 cup florets of cauliflower
2 tbsp finely grated carrots
2 tbsp finely chopped red cabbage
1 tbsp roundels of yellow squash
1 cup finely shredded cabbage or lettuce
2 tbsp vinegar
2 tbsp oil
1 large onion, grated
2 tbsp mayonnaise

- Steam broccoli and cauliflower.
- Combine with other vegetables and mix thoroughly with vinegar.
- In a small pan heat oil, add onion and sauté until they begin to soften.
- Add to the vegetables. Also add mayonnaise. Mix and serve.

ENERGY SALAD

Serves 6

2 cups shredded lettuce (iceberg in season)
1 cup coarsely chopped spinach
½ cup sliced cucumber
½ cup sliced tomatoes
½ cup sprouted green gram (sabut moong) or wheat
½ cup grated carrot
3 tbsp oil
3 tbsp fresh lime juice
½ tsp salt
¼ tsp ground black pepper

- Put all the salad ingredients into a large bowl.
- Whip together the oil, lime juice, salt and pepper and pour over the salad. Mix and serve.

CURRIED GREEN JACKFRUIT (KATHAL)

Serves 6-8

1 kg green jackfruit (kathal)
4 potatoes
2 tbsp oil
¼ tsp cumin seeds
½ tsp sugar

For paste:

3 dry red chillies
1 tbsp cumin seeds
1 tbsp coriander seeds
½ tsp turmeric powder
Salt to taste
1½ cups water

For tempering:

1 tbsp ghee
2-3 bay leaves
1 tsp garam masala powder

· Peel the outer skin of jackfruit. Remove seeds, if any. Also throw away the fibrous portion of the jackfruit, retaining only the 'meaty' portion. There is a layer of skin between the seed and the fruit. Ensure that this is also removed and thrown away.

· Cut jackfruit into bite-size (or a little larger) pieces. Place in a pan with water and boil for approximately 15 minutes. Remove from fire. Drain well.

· Peel and cut potatoes into 1" cubes.

· Heat oil in a kadhai. Fry potatoes until lightly

browned. Remove from pan.

· Sauté the spices and make into paste along with salt and water.

· Add paste and sugar to the pan. Stir well and fry for several minutes, sprinkling water when necessary. Continue stirring and frying until masala changes colour.

· Add 1½ cups water, stir and add the boiled kathal and potato. Simmer gently until the potato and kathal are both cooked and there is gravy in the pan.

· In a separate pan or kadhai, heat the ghee. Add the bay leaves and whole cumin seeds. Stir-fry until the masala stops spluttering. Pour onto the vegetables and sprinkle garam masala. Stir well and cook for 1 minute.

· Serve hot with rice or chapatti.

GREEN PAPAYA CURRY

Serves 6

500 gm green papaya, peeled and cut into small pieces
2 tbsp ghee
2 bay leaves
¼ tsp onion seeds (kalonji)
2 green chillies, chopped
Salt to taste

For paste:

2 bay leaves
1½ tbsp coriander seeds
¼ tsp turmeric powder
½ tbsp cumin seeds

- Boil the green papaya in enough water to cover for about 10 minutes. Drain the water, discard and set papaya aside.

- In a kadhai, heat 1½ tbsp ghee. Add the bay leaves and onion seeds and stir-fry for half a minute. Now add boiled papaya, stir, and add the paste and salt to taste. Cover and cook for about 5 minutes.

- Remove cover, add green chillies and continue cooking, stirring from time to time until all the water from the papaya has evaporated. If papaya is not quite cooked, add a little water.

- Add ½ tbsp ghee. Stir it in and remove from fire.

MANGA PACHADI

Mango and Curd Salad

Serves 6

2 tsp corn oil
1 tsp brown mustard seeds
2 small green mangoes, skinned and finely chopped
2 cups curd
Salt to taste

For paste:

2 tbsp freshly grated coconut
2 green chillies, finely chopped

For tempering:

1 tsp cumin seeds
1 dry red chilli, broken
1 sprig curry leaves

- Heat 1 tsp corn oil, add mustard seeds. When they pop, add mango.

- Grind coconut and chillies to a fine paste and add to mango. Fry for 3 minutes, then take off fire. Transfer to a bowl.

- Beat curd with salt and mix with mango.

- Heat remaining oil in a pan and add the tempering ingredients. When mustard seeds splutter, pour into the bowl and mix.

This is served as a side dish with rice, dal and vegetables. In southern India the most delicious salads are made with curd, using cooked vegetables and tempering. They are excellent summer food and ideal for visitors from abroad who feel uncomfortable eating uncooked food. Even the curd should be made at home in this case.

ARABI SOOKHI

Colocassia Dry

Serves 6

1 kg colocassia (arabi)
2 tbsp oil
⅛ tsp asafoetida powder
1 tsp mustard seeds
1 dry red chilli
½ tsp turmeric powder
Salt to taste
1 tsp Bengal gram (chana dal), washed
1 tsp black gram (urad dal), washed

· Pressure cook arabi for 10 minutes or until done properly.

· Peel and chop into ¾" pieces.

· Heat oil and add all spices and dals, except turmeric.

· When the mustard seeds pop, add arabi with turmeric and salt.

· Stir-fry, making sure that all sides are browned. Stir gently.

· When brown, remove from fire.

· Serve hot with chapatti and dal.

ARABI CUTLET

Colocassia Cutlet

Serves 6

500 gm small colocassia (arabi)
½ tsp turmeric powder
1 tsp coriander powder
1 tsp cumin powder
¼ tsp chilli powder
A little less than ¼ tsp ajwain
1 tsp dried mango powder (amchur)
Salt to taste
2 tbsp oil

- Wash arabi.
- Pressure cook for 10 minutes. Remove and run under cold water.
- Peel skin.
- Press in the palm of the hand and flatten.
- Mix all spices together with salt. Press arabi into the spices, coating it fully.
- Heat oil in a kadhai and add arabi. Fry till light brown and sprinkle any remaining spice mixture on top.
- Sprinkle water delicately to prevent burning of the spices and fry until a darkish brown.
- Serve hot with chapatti.

GREEN CHICKPEAS CABBAGE AND TOMATOES RASEDAR

Serves 6

1 small cabbage
4 tomatoes
2 cups green chickpeas (hara cholia)
1 tsp salt
2 tsp oil
1 pinch asafoetida powder
3 green chillies, slit
½ tsp cumin powder
¼ tsp chilli powder
½ tsp turmeric powder

- Cut cabbage thinly and quarter the tomatoes.

- Boil water in a large pot, add chickpeas and ½ tsp salt. Boil uncovered for 5 minutes if chickpeas are tender. If large and mature, cook for 20 minutes. Drain and set aside.

- Heat oil in a kadhai. Add asafoetida, chickpeas, green chillies, all the spices and stir-fry for 5 minutes.

- Add cabbage and toss together, stir-frying for 2 minutes.

- Add tomatoes on top. Lower flame. Cover and cook for 5 minutes. Remove lid and mix together.

- You will get a medley of colours and a delicious flavour.

HARA CHOLIA JABARDAST
Delicious Green Chickpeas

Serves 4

Ask your local vegetable vendor to get fresh young green chickpeas shelled for you. They cost a bomb, but are worth it.

2 tbsp oil
1 pinch asafoetida powder
3 cups young, fresh chickpeas (hara cholia)
½ tsp cumin powder
1 level tsp salt
2 fresh red chillies, chopped in thin roundels
1 tsp sesame seeds, roasted

- Heat oil in a kadhai. Add asafoetida.

- Add fresh chickpeas, sprinkle cumin powder and salt.

- Stir-fry for 3 minutes, then add red chillies and sesame seeds. Fry for 2 minutes more.

- Sprinkle water generously.

- Cover, lower flame and simmer for 5 minutes.

- This can be served as a savoury with drinks or tea or even as a vegetable dish.

Lentils, Pulses and Beans

We used to say *khaiye dal jerdi nibai nal*, eat lentils which everyone can afford. Farmers always grow some dal, beans and peas for their daily fare. The rich and the poor vegetarians get their requisite intake of proteins from lentils. Every Indian, when away from home, misses his dal whether it is sambar, rasam, dal makhani or ambat, for each region has a different way of making dal. The Punjabis make it thick and generously tempered with pure ghee and spices. The people of Uttar Pradesh generally make hulled dals of a thin consistency and flavour it delicately with spices. In Rajasthan, it is the rich chana dal or hulled black gram, eaten with a lot of chillies and ghee. Maharashtrians make a wonderful ambat with tamarind and jaggery. South of the Vindhyas, sambar made from toor dal, and rasam are an essential part of the meal. The most complex way of making dal is the Parsi speciality of dhansak. Any Parsi cookbook or family will give you a recipe. They feel that is the only way dal should be eaten!

The former Nawab of Rampur had a cook whose speciality was all types of dal. The cook boasted that he could make dals *ek hazar ek tarike se*, in one thousand and one ways.

DHULI MOONG DAL

Hulled Lentils

Serves 6

1½ cups green gram (moong dhuli, split and hulled)
½ tsp turmeric powder
¼ tsp chilli powder
¼ tsp black pepper
2 cloves garlic, peeled
2 pieces ginger, 1" square
1½ tsp salt
1½ tbsp lime juice

For tempering:

3 tbsp vegetable oil or ghee
1 pinch asafoetida powder
1 tsp cumin seeds

· Clean and wash dal thoroughly. Place in heavy-bottomed pan and add 4 cups water. Bring to a boil. Remove the froth and scum that collects at the top. Now add turmeric, chilli and pepper and cook.

· Make a paste of ginger and garlic in a blender and add. Cook covered, leaving the lid very slightly ajar. Lower heat, and simmer gently for about 20 minutes. Stir occasionally. When dal is cooked, add the salt and lime juice.

· The dal should be creamy.

· In a small pot, preferably an iron kadhai, heat the vegetable oil or ghee over a medium flame. When hot, add asafoetida. As soon as the asafoetida sizzles, add cumin seeds. When the seeds turn dark, pour the oil and spices over the dal.

Take dal off the fire and set aside, covered. The Bengali cook adds 2 to 3 washed leaves of *gandho raj* (lime) leaves and closes the lid. The leaves should never be cooked for the dal will become bitter. If you wish to reheat the dal, remove the leaves.

According to naturopaths moong dal split and hulled is the easiest food to digest and is also non-toxic.

CHILKA MOONG

Mashed Green Dal

Serves 6

1 cup green gram (moong dal), split but not hulled
½ tsp turmeric powder
Salt to taste
1 lime-sized lump of tamarind, soaked in ½ cup hot water for 1 hour
4 green chillies, slit lengthwise

For tempering:

2 tsp pure ghee or butter
¼ tsp asafoetida powder
1 dry red chilli, split
1 tsp brown mustard seeds
1 sprig curry leaves
1 onion (optional)

· Clean, wash and drain dal.

· Put in pressure cooker, add 3 cups water and boil.
Add turmeric and salt. Cook for 10 minutes under
pressure. Cool, open and add tamarind paste and
green chillies. Cook covered for 10 minutes, stirring
constantly and mashing the mixture.

· Heat ghee and add asafoetida. When it sizzles, add
dry red chilli, mustard and curry leaves. When it
splutters, add to dal, stirring until everything blends.

· For decoration and flavour (optional), use one onion
thinly sliced lengthwise and browned in oil.

· Serve hot, with browned onions sprinkled on top.

MOONG DAL DOSAI

Hulled Lentil Pancakes

Serves 6

2 cups green gram (moong dal), split
½ cup rice
3 green chillies, chopped
1 large onion, finely chopped
3 tbsp chopped green coriander
Salt to taste
3 tbsp oil for shallow frying

- Clean and wash dal and soak with rice in 2 cups water for 1 hour.

- Drain in a fine colander.

- Put in a blender with chopped green chillies and blend into a coarse paste.

- Place batter in a container and mix all other ingredients in it.

- Heat a griddle. To test that it is ready, sprinkle a few drops of water; if the water sizzles, it is ready.

- Put a little oil and using a cut potato, smear it all over the griddle.

- Pour a ladle full of batter into the centre of the griddle and move the ladle in a circular movement outwards as for making a thin pancake.

- Make a dent in the centre of the dosai with the back of the ladle.

- Pour ½ tsp oil in the middle and ½ tsp around. Cook until golden brown on both sides and crisp.
- Serve hot with coconut chutney.

LENTIL WAFFLES

Makes 8-9

1½ cups green gram (moong dal), split
1 tsp baking powder
3 tbsp corn oil
1 tsp salt
½ tsp cumin powder
¼ tsp chilli powder
2 tbsp yoghurt
1 tbsp dried fenugreek leaves, soaked in water

- Wash dal well and soak in water for 2 hours.
- Put soaked dal with water in liquidizer and add all ingredients except fenugreek. Grind to a paste. Remove from liquidizer and add water, if necessary, for pouring consistency.
- Drain water from fenugreek and mix into the paste thoroughly. Keep for 1 hour.
- Heat teflon waffle maker for 5 minutes. Open and pour one ladle of the mixture. Spread with wooden spatula and close. Cook for 5 minutes, till crisp on both sides.
- Remove from the waffle maker and keep covered with a napkin, then start the next.

This is an ideal breakfast food. You can keep the waffle maker on the table and make it as you eat. The first waffle takes 5 minutes but after that it takes less time. For those who have an allergy to wheat or gluten this is a life-saver.

MILLI-JULLI DAL DOSAI

Mixed Lentil Pancake

Serves 6

½ cup husked black gram (urad dal)
½ cup pigeon peas (toor/arhar dal)
½ cup Bengal gram (chana dal)
1 cup rice
4 dry red chillies
5 tbsp coconut flakes
Salt to taste

· Clean and wash all dals and rice and soak with chillies in 2 cups water for 2 hours.

· Drain thoroughly and mix in a blender, adding water, if necessary, so as to get a flowing paste.

· Combine with coconut and salt in a container.

· Cover and set aside for 2 to 3 hours.

· Make dosai as given in recipe for moong dal dosai (p. 244).

MOONG DAL CHUTNEY

Lentil Chutney

½ cup green gram (moong dal)
2 tbsp oil
2 dry red chillies
1 small green mango, grated, or juice of 2 limes
4 tbsp freshly grated coconut
Salt to taste

- Clean, wash and drain dal.
- In a small kadhai heat oil, saute dal and chillies until the dal is fried a golden brown colour.
- Cool dal and put into a blender with all the other ingredients. Add 2 to 3 tbsp water as required and blend into a paste. Add salt to taste.

This is delicious with crisp parantha and with hot rice and melted butter.

CHANA DAL AUR GHIA

Bengal Gram with Bottle Gourd

Serves 4

½ cup Bengal gram (chana dal)
Salt to taste
500 gm bottle gourd
4 dried lime (leemu Ommani) (optional)

For tempering:

2 tbsp ghee or butter
1 dry red chilli, broken
¼ tsp black mustard seeds
½ tsp cumin seeds
10 fenugreek seeds
2 green chillies, chopped

· Clean, wash and drain dal.

· Put dal with 3 cups water in a pressure cooker. Add ½ tsp salt. Cook for 20 minutes.

· Peel bottle gourd and cut into half, removing pulp and seeds. Cut into ½" pieces, add water and cook for 10 to 15 minutes without pressure until the ghia is cooked and soft. Set aside.

· If available, add leemu Ommani along with ghia, for a sour taste. This is a very special Persian condiment used in *queemy*, a dish made with dal and lamb.

· In a kadhai, heat ghee over a medium flame. When hot, add red chilli, mustard, cumin, and fenugreek seeds. In a few seconds, as soon as the cumin and fenugreek seeds darken and mustard seeds begin to pop, add green chillies. Turn them over once and quickly add to dal.

Mix well and cook over medium flame for 3 minutes, stirring frequently but gently.

SABUT URAD AUR RAJMAH DAL

Black Gram and Kidney Beans

Serves 6

1 cup black gram (urad dal)
½ cup kidney beans (rajmah), washed
1" piece ginger, peeled and sliced
8 cloves garlic, peeled
5 tbsp curd
¼ tsp chilli powder
1¾ tsp salt
¼ tsp freshly ground pepper

For tempering:

3 tbsp oil or pure ghee
1 pinch asafoetida powder
½ tsp cumin seeds
2 red dry chillies
1" ginger, peeled and grated coarsely

- Clean and wash dal and rajmah and soak overnight.

- In a pressure cooker put the drained dal and rajmah with 5 cups water, ginger and garlic. Cook for 25 minutes. Check that the rajmah and dal are soft. If not, pressure cook further for 5 minutes.

- Put the curd in a small bowl. Beat well with a fork and set aside.

- After the dal has cooked, mash well against the sides of the pot with the back of a ladle. Pour in the curd, stirring as you do, then add the chilli powder, salt and pepper. Return to fire and bring to a boil, cover, lower heat, and simmer for 10 minutes.

· For tempering, heat oil or ghee in a kadhai. Put asafoetida, cumin and red chillies. Add ginger and sauté for 1 minute. Add the contents to the cooked dal and close lid.

· Serve hot with chapatis or boiled rice.

SABUT MASOOR DAL PIAZ

Whole Egyptian Lentils with Onions

Serves 4-6

1½ cups Egyptian lentils (masoor dal, sabut)
2 tsp oil
¼ tsp asafoetida powder
½ tsp turmeric paste
1 tsp chilli paste
10-12 small pearl onions, peeled
Salt to taste

For tempering:

1 tbsp ghee
1 large onion, finely sliced
½ tsp garam masala powder
1 tsp chopped green coriander

· Soak dal in water for 4 hours or overnight. Drain.
  Spread dal thinly in a large thali or plate and leave
  until half dry.

· In a kadhai or pan heat oil. Add asafoetida, turmeric
  and chilli paste. Fry for a few seconds, then add dal.
  Stir well.

· Fry dal over medium heat, stirring all the while.
  When dal begins to change colour, add the pearl
  onions and continue frying. Add salt at this stage.

· Keep handy approximately 2 cups water and sprinkle
  a little at a time over the dal so that it does not stick to
  the bottom of the pan. Add salt to taste.

· Continue frying the dal, sprinkling water a little at a

time, as required, so that finally the dal is cooked but still remains whole and there is practically no gravy. The dal is done when it mashes easily between finger and thumb. Remove from fire.

· Heat ghee in a small frying pan, add sliced onions and sauté till brown.

· Add garam masala and fry for half a minute.

· Pour over the dal and mix.

· Serve with green coriander sprinkled on top.

Caution is necessary when adding water. It must be sprinkled with the fingers; if too much water is added, the dal becomes a lump. The dal must be soft to the touch but remain whole. This is a time-consuming process and I would advise that you try it only if you have a lot of time and are a patient cook.

MASOOR DAL SALAD

Egyptian Lentil Salad

Serves 6

200 gm Egyptian lentils (masoor dal)
2 capsicums, cut into thin, long pieces
1 onion, finely sliced
1 bunch green coriander, chopped
½ cup French dressing with 1 tsp chilli sauce

Boil masoor dal until it splits and becomes soft. Drain. The water can be reserved for use in soups.

Mix all the ingredients.

Refrigerate before serving.

EGYPTIAN LENTIL SOUP

Serves 6

2 cups Egyptian lentils (masoor dal)
1 large onion, finely chopped
8 cloves garlic, finely chopped
2 sticks cinnamon
4 large black cardamoms
2 bay leaves
2 dry red chillies
2 tsp cumin powder
1½ tbsp lime juice
2 sprigs fresh mint
Salt to taste
1 lime, sliced into wedges

- Clean, wash and drain dal. Put into pressure cooker and add 6 cups water. Add onion, garlic, cinnamon, cardamoms, bay leaves, dry chillies, salt and 1½ tsp cumin powder. Pressure cook for 20 minutes.

- Cool and open lid. The dal should be cooked thoroughly. Mix together and taste for salt. Cook dal without lid for 10 minutes so that the water and dal get mixed together. Remove cinnamon, cardamom, bay leaves and red chillies and discard.

- Add lime juice and stir. The consistency should be that of a thick soup. If too thick, add water and cook for 5 minutes.

- Serve hot in individual bowls with a sprinkling of cumin powder, a sprig of mint and a wedge of lime.

DAL PAALAK

Lentils and Spinach

Serves 6

1 cup Bengal gram (chana dal)
1 stick cinnamon
2 large black cardamoms
1 tsp peppercorns
500 gm spinach cleaned, washed and finely chopped
Salt to taste

For tempering:

2 tsp ghee
1 red dry chilli, broken
¼ tsp asafoetida powder
1 tsp cumin seeds
1" ginger, grated
5 cloves garlic, finely chopped

- Clean and wash dal and put in a pressure cooker with 4 cups water along with spices. Pressure cook for 20 minutes.

- Remove from fire, cool and open. Add spinach and salt to taste. Cover and cook without pressure for 10 minutes.

- In a tiny kadhai heat ghee, add chilli, asafoetida and cumin seeds. Stir for half a minute.

- Add ginger and garlic and stir-fry for 1 minute. Pour the contents into the dal.

- Close lid. Serve the dal hot.

MASOOR OR ARHAR DAL WITH SABZI

Lentils with Vegetables

Serves 6-8

2 cups Egyptian lentils (masoor dal) or pigeon peas (toor/arhar dal)
3 dry red chillies
½ tsp turmeric powder
3 tbsp chopped green coriander
1 medium-sized bottle gourd/pumpkin/aubergine
Salt to taste
2 walnut-sized lumps of tamarind, soaked in water

For tempering:

3 tbsp vegetable oil or ghee
10 black peppercorns
½ tsp cumin seeds
½ tsp black mustard seeds

- Clean and wash dal and put in a pressure cooker with 4 cups water and bring to a boil. If there is any scum, remove it with a spoon. Add red chillies, turmeric and coriander and cover. Close lid and pressure cook for 15 minutes.

- Wash the vegetable and cut into ¾" pieces.

- Remove lid and add salt, vegetable, tamarind paste and sugar. Add 1 cup hot water if required. Cook for 8 minutes more in pressure cooker.

- Remove from fire and set aside. Open lid and simmer for 5 minutes without lid.

- In an iron kadhai heat oil and add all the spices for

tempering. When the mustard seeds begin to pop, pour some of the dal into the kadhai, mixing with the tempering. Blend well together.

- Serve hot.

NARIAL SABZI DAL

Dal with Vegetable and Coconut

Serves 6

½ cup pigeon peas (toor/arhar dal), washed
1 lime-sized lump of tamarind, soaked in 1½ cups warm water
2 tbsp oil
½ cup chopped onion
1 long brinjal, cut into pieces
1 potato, peeled and cut
1 capsicum, cut
½ tsp turmeric powder
Salt to taste

For paste:

1 tsp corn oil
1 tsp cumin seeds
3 tbsp coriander seeds
4 dry red chillies
¼ tsp asafoetida powder
½ tbsp Bengal gram (chana dal), washed
½ coconut, freshly grated, or 8 tbsp flaked coconut

For tempering:

2 tbsp corn oil
¼ tsp fenugreek seeds
1 tsp cumin seeds
1 dry red chilli, broken
1 sprig curry leaves
¼ cup thinly-sliced onions

For garnishing:

3 tbsp chopped green coriander

· Clean and wash toor dal and pressure cook for 15

minutes. Set aside.

· Mix tamarind with water, strain and set aside.

· Heat 1 tsp oil, sauté for 2 minutes all the ingredients for the paste, except coconut.

· Add coconut to the sautéed spices and mix to a paste, adding very little water. Set aside.

· Heat 2 tbsp oil in a pan. Add chopped onion and sauté till golden. Now add the vegetables, turmeric and salt, stir together briskly and sauté for 2 minutes. Sprinkle a little water and cover. Cook over low fire for 3 minutes.

· Add cooked dal with the water and paste and mix together. If too thick, add ¼ to ½ cup hot water and simmer until the vegetables are cooked.

· Heat 2 tsp oil and add the spices for tempering as well as curry leaves. When seeds splutter, add onion and sauté for 4 to 5 minutes. Pour over the dal and vegetable and close lid.

· Serve hot, mixing in the green coriander.

MOONG DHULI SABZI

Green Gram with Vegetables

Serves 6-8

1 cup hulled green gram (moong dhuli)
2 cups mixed vegetables, 1" cubes or cut lengthwise
(combination of cauliflower, radish, marrow, parmal, flat beans,
potato, drumstick and peas)
1 walnut-sized lump of tamarind, soaked and juice extracted
6-8 green chillies, slit
Salt to taste

For paste:

2 dry red chillies
1 tsp coriander seeds
2 tbsp cumin seeds
1 tbsp grated ginger
Salt to taste

For tempering:

1 tbsp ghee
½ tsp panch phoron

- Clean, wash and drain dal. Add to four cups of boiling water in a pan and cook on a medium fire for 10 minutes.

- Add vegetables according to the time taken to cook. Potato, drumstick and radish take longer to cook.

- Blend ingedients for paste and add to vegetables. Mix well and simmer over medium fire for 10 minutes.

- Add other vegetables to dal according to their cooking time. When the vegetables are nearly done, add tamarind and, finally, the slit green chillies and salt.

· Mix thoroughly and simmer for another 5 minutes or until all vegetables are tender.

Tempering:
· In a kadhai, heat ghee and add panch phoron. When the spices start popping, add to the dal. Stir, bring the dal to a boil and remove from fire.

THAIR SAMBAR

Buttermilk Sambar

Serves 6

1 tsp pigeon peas (toor/arhar dal)
1 tsp Bengal gram (chana dal)
½" piece ginger, finely grated
1 tsp cumin seeds
1 tbsp coriander seeds
4 green chillies
½ tsp turmeric powder
3 tbsp freshly grated coconut or 4 tsp flaked dry coconut
2 cups plain curd
Salt to taste
1 cup petha or ash gourd, peeled and cubed into ½" pieces

For tempering:

2 tsp oil
1 tsp brown mustard seeds
¼ tsp fenugreek seeds
1 dry red chilli
¼ tsp asafoetida powder
1 sprig curry leaves

- Clean and wash dals and soak in water for 2 hours and then drain.
- Put dals, ginger, spices and coconut in a blender and make into a paste with very little water.
- Mix the paste with curd, add salt and set aside.
- Heat 2 tsp oil in a pan. Add all the ingredients for tempering.

- When the mustard seeds pop, add ash gourd.

- Put in 3 cups water to cover vegetable. Bring to a boil. Cover. Lower heat and simmer on a low fire until cooked. Remove from fire.

- Before serving, heat the vegetable mixture. Remove from fire, add curd mixture to vegetable, stirring slowly. Replace and reduce flame. Stir while heating. The mixture must not boil, otherwise it may curdle.

This is a delicious dish to be eaten with rice in the hot season.

SMALL ONION SAMBAR

Serves 6

½ cup pigeon peas (toor/arhar dal)
1 lime-sized lump of tamarind, soaked in 1½ cups warm water
½ tsp turmeric powder
Salt to taste

For paste:

2 tsp corn oil
4 dry red chillies
¼ tsp asafoetida powder
1 tsp cumin seeds
3 tbsp coriander seeds
½ tbsp Bengal gram (chana dal), washed
2 large onions, chopped
4 tbsp freshly grated coconut or 6 tbsp flaked dry coconut

For tempering:

2 tbsp corn oil
½ tsp fenugreek seeds
1 tsp mustard seeds
1 dry red chilli, broken
1 sprig curry leaves
250 gm small onions, peeled

For garnishing:

3 tbsp chopped green coriander

- Clean and wash toor dal and pressure cook with 3 cups water for 20 minutes.

- Mix tamarind with water, strain and set pulp aside.

- Heat 2 tsp oil and sauté for 2 minutes all the spices for the paste along with chana dal. Blend with chopped

266

onion and coconut, adding very little water. Set
aside.

· Heat 2 tsp oil in a pan, add the spices and curry leaves
for tempering. When seeds splutter, add small onions
and sauté for 4 to 5 minutes.

· Add tamarind, turmeric powder and salt, stir
together briskly, and sauté for 2 minutes. Add ½ cup
water and cover. Cook over low fire for 3 minutes.

· Add dal to the water and masala paste and mix
together. If too thick, add ¼ to ½ cup of hot water
and bring to a boil.

· Serve hot, mixing in the green coriander.

AMCHIGELAI SAMBAR

Saraswat Brahmin Sambar

Serves 6

¾ cup pigeon peas (toor/arhar dal)
Salt to taste
1 potato, peeled and cut into pieces
½ cup shelled peas
250 gm string beans, chopped
½ tsp turmeric powder
2 walnut-sized lumps of tamarind, soaked in 1 cup water

For paste:

1 tbsp coriander seeds
½ coconut, grated
1 tsp rice
6 dry red chillies
¼ tsp asafoetida powder

For tempering:

2 tsp oil
1 tsp mustard seeds
1 tsp cumin seeds
1 dry red chilli, broken
1 sprig curry leaves

- Clean and wash dal and pressure cook with 3 cups water and salt for 15 minutes.

- Mix all the ingredients for the paste in a blender with very little water and set aside.

- Put all vegetables in a pan and pour enough water to cover them. Cook until tender.

- Add vegetables to dal together with the water,

268

turmeric and paste.

- Strain tamarind, discard pulp and add. Mix together and simmer, stirring until all the ingredients are well blended.

- Cook on very low fire for 5 to 7 minutes.

- Heat 2 tsp oil in an iron kadhai and add mustard seeds, cumin seeds, red chilli and curry leaves. When the mustard seeds pop, add the mixture to the sambar and close lid.

- Serve the sambar piping hot with boiled rice.

Amchigelai means 'our people'. My friend Usha, who is a wonderful cook, cooks the most delicious dishes of the Saraswat Brahmin community. *Batata Sang*, hot potatoes, *ambat, sar* and this special sambar. The people of Mangalore have the most delicious cuisine with a number of chutneys, pickles and seafood dishes.

LOBIA TARIDAR

Black-eyed Beans Curry

Serves 6

1 cup black-eyed dry beans (lobia)
2 tbsp oil
¼ tsp asafoetida powder
3 onions, finely chopped
6 cloves garlic, finely chopped
½ tsp turmeric powder
1 tsp coriander powder
1 tsp cumin powder
1 tsp garam masala powder
3 tomatoes, peeled and chopped
1 tsp salt
1 bunch coriander leaves

Clean, wash and soak beans for 2 hours. Drain and set aside.

· Heat oil in a pressure cooker. Add asafoetida and stir. Add onion and fry until transparent. Add garlic and stir-fry for 1 minute. Add all the spices except garam masala and stir-fry for half a minute.

· Add tomatoes and mix thoroughly, frying for a minute.

· Now add the beans and stir-fry for 3 minutes.

· If necessary, sprinkle water so that the spices do not burn.

· Add 3 cups water and salt. Close lid and pressure cook for 20 minutes. Cool and check if beans are cooked properly and soft. Add garam masala.

· Simmer uncovered for 3 minutes.

· Serve hot with a sprinkling of chopped coriander leaves.

c h i c k p e a s

Chickpeas or chana form an important part of the Indian diet. We have the white chickpeas, known as *kabuli chana* which, as the name suggests, possibly came from Afghanistan. It is treated as a delicacy and greatly loved. Then we have the *kala chana*, the black chickpeas, which are indigenous to India, are commonly eaten. The split black chickpeas make *chana dal*. Ground chana made into flour—*besan*—is used for making savouries like *pakoras*, fried fritters, the Gujarati dish *khandvi, besan ki roti*—flat bread eaten by diabetics. It is also used for thickening dishes made from buttermilk.

Chickpeas are also greatly appreciated in the Arab world and in the Middle East. Hummus, made from chickpeas, is one of the most versatile dishes known all over the world. It is seasoned with sesame. In Egypt and Middle

East *tahina* or sesame paste is available and is mixed with hummus to make *hummus bi tahina*.

I roast sesame seeds, which are half the quantity of chickpeas, set aside 1 tsp sesame seeds and crush the rest into a paste and blend the two together. Before serving, the whole sesame seeds are sprinkled on top.

The most delicious of all is the fresh green chana, juicy and succulent. As a child, I remember buying green chanas, which came on a stem in thick bunches. My friends and I would roast them on an open fire in the chill of winter and then crack the pods to eat them. We were forbidden to light a fire in the absence of adult supervision. But who could resist it? Our faces, hands and clothes would become black with the burnt chanas and we would sneak into the house trying to wash away all evidence.

The green chickpeas have always remained my favourite and I have improvised a number of dishes ranging from salad, pulao to soups and vegetables.

CHICKPEA SALAD

Serves 6

250 gm white chickpeas (kabuli chana)
1½ tsp salt
200 gm spring onions, chopped
1 small cabbage, finely shredded
¼ cup chopped mint
¾ cup French dressing
¼ tsp chilli powder

- Soak chickpeas overnight and discard the water. Wash once again.

- Put chickpeas in a pressure cooker and pour water 1" above the level of chickpeas. Add 1 tsp salt. Pressure cook for 20 minutes.

- Check if the chickpeas are done. If not, pressure cook for 5 minutes more.

- Drain and reserve liquid as stock.

- Mix all the ingredients together. Toss together. I prefer to toss the salad with my hands.

- Serve in a wooden bowl.

HUMMUS: CHICKPEA SPREAD

200 gm white chickpeas (kabuli chana)
8 cloves garlic, finely crushed
3 tsp cumin powder
3 tbsp olive oil
¼ tsp chilli powder
3 tbsp lime juice
Salt and black pepper to taste

- Cook chickpeas as for Chickpea Salad (p. 274).
- Mix all ingredients and run through liquidizer.
- Refrigerate in a jar.
- Serve in a platter with a little extra oil on top.

My version of hummus has ¼ cup mint leaves added to the ingredients and then puréed. Hummus can be served with mint leaves on the side.

I also add 100 gm white sesame seeds roasted on a griddle. The sesame seeds are pounded in a pestle, reserving 1 tbsp for garnish. The ground sesame is mixed with chickpeas and blended together. The garnish is sprinkled on top before serving.

KABULI CHANA AUR GUCHI

Chickpeas with Black Mushroom

Serves 6

100 gm black mushrooms
200 gm white chickpeas (kabuli chana), boiled
10 cloves garlic, peeled and chopped
1 piece of ginger, 2" long and 1" wide, peeled and chopped
¼ tsp asafoetida powder
½ tsp turmeric powder
¼ cup tomato purée
4 medium-sized potatoes, freshly boiled, peeled and chopped
1½ tsp salt
½ tsp freshly ground black pepper
½ tsp chilli powder
2 tbsp lime juice

- Soak mushrooms in hot water 2 hours before cooking or overnight. Remove from water and cut into long pieces.

- Cook chickpeas as for Chickpea Salad (p. 274).

- Blend garlic and ginger into a paste with 2 tbsp water.

- Heat oil in a heavy-bottomed pan over a medium flame and put in the asafoetida. After a few seconds, add the garlic and ginger paste. Add turmeric, stir-fry for half a minute. Add tomato puree and pour in 1 cup water and stir.

- Now add drained chickpeas and potato. Put in the salt, black pepper and chilli powder. Bring to a boil.

· Add mushroom to the mixture, combining together gently. Cook for 10 minutes on low heat. Add lime juice.

These chickpeas taste good with rice and chapatti. Serve curd and chutney as accompaniment.

KALA CHANA AUR ALU RASEDAR

Black Chickpea and Potato Curry

Serves 4

200 gm black chickpeas (kala chana)
1½ tsp salt
1 tsp bicarbonate of soda
3 tbsp vegetable oil
¼ tsp asafoetida powder
½ tsp cumin seeds
4 medium-sized potatoes, peeled and cubed
1 tsp coriander powder
1 tsp garam masala powder
½ tsp chilli powder

For paste:

1 medium-sized onion, peeled and chopped
6 cloves garlic, peeled and chopped
1 piece ginger, about 1" square, peeled and chopped

- Soak chana overnight. Discard water and wash thoroughly.

- Put chana in a pressure cooker. Add 1 tsp salt, bicarbonate of soda, pour water 1" above the level of chana. Cover and pressure cook for 20 minutes. If the chana is not soft, cook for 5 minutes more. Check on water level. Drain the chana and reserve liquid.

- Put onion, garlic and ginger in a blender with 3 tbsp water and make into smooth paste.

- In a pan heat the oil over a medium flame. When very

278

hot, put in asafoetida and cumin seeds. After a few seconds, when the cumin darkens, put in the paste from the blender. Fry, stirring until the oil is separated, for approximately 5 minutes.

· Add chana, salt and turmeric and stir-fry. Put in the potato, coriander, garam masala, chilli power and stir-fry for 2 minutes. Add 2 cups reserved liquid and cover. Lower heat and simmer for 10-12 minutes until potatoes are done.

· Stir. Check salt. Cook for 10 minutes without lid, stirring occasionally.

KABULI CHANA MASALEDAR

Spiced White Chickpeas

Serves 6

200 gm white chickpeas (kabuli chana)
3 tbsp vegetable oil
1 tsp cumin seeds
1 medium-sized onion, peeled and chopped
¼ tsp ground cinnamon
¼ tsp ground nutmeg
¼ tsp ground cloves
1 tsp ground coriander
2 cloves garlic, peeled and minced
2" piece ginger, grated
1 tbsp tomato paste
1 tsp salt
¼ tsp chilli powder
1 tbsp dried mango powder (amchur)

For garnishing:
1" ginger cut into thin, long slices and soaked in 2 tbsp
lime juice and ¼ tsp salt
A few wedges of lime

- Soak chickpeas overnight and cook as for Chickpea Salad (p. 274).

- Drain and reserve liquid.

- Heat oil in a heavy-bottomed pan over medium flame. Put in the cumin seeds. As soon as they begin to darken, add the chopped onion. Stir-fry for 2 minutes or until onion begins to turn a golden brown.

· Lower heat and add the cinnamon, nutmeg, clove and coriander and stir-fry for half a minute. Add the garlic and grated ginger and fry, stirring, for 2 to 3 minutes. Add the tomato paste and fry for 1 minute.

· Pour the chickpeas into the pan and stir-fry for 3 minutes. In ½ cup reserved liquid mix salt, chilli powder and amchur. Blend well. Cover and let the chickpeas cook with the spices for about 10 minutes. Stir gently every now and then, taking care not to break the chickpeas.

· Serve piping hot with the sliced ginger sprinkled on top and with wedges of lime.

KALA CHANA SHORBA

Black Chickpea Soup

A healthy soup for everyone, specially those who need to recoup their energy.

Serves 6

1 cup black chickpeas (kala chana)
1 large onion, finely chopped
1 tsp salt
1 tsp black pepper
1 tsp bicarbonate of soda
1 pinch asafoetida powder
1 tbsp lime juice

- Clean and wash chana and soak overnight. If black chickpeas are not available, use white chickpeas.

- Rinse again and put in a pressure cooker with onion, salt, pepper, bicarbonate of soda and asafoetida. Add 8 cups water and pressure cook. After 20 minutes check the chana for softness. If necessary, cook for 10 minutes more in the pressure cooker until soft.

- Run half the chana through a liquidizer and keep the other half whole.

- After liquidizing, mix them all together and simmer for 10 minutes.

- Add lime juice and serve.

BLACK CHIKPEA SOUP AU-GRATIN

Serves 6

1 cup black chickpeas (kala chana)
3 slices wholewheat bread
2 large onions, finely sliced
1 tsp bicarbonate of soda
1 tbsp butter
2 tbsp grated Parmesan
¼ tsp paprika

- Cook according to the recipe for black chickpea soup (p. 282). When the soup is ready, set aside.

- Toast the bread crisp, cut into bite-size pieces and set aside.

- In a pan fry the onion in butter and add to the soup.

- Just before serving, warm the soup, put it in heat-proof soup bowls and add the pieces of toast to each bowl.

- Sprinkle Parmesan and a pinch of paprika on top.

- Put into oven with the top griller on.

- Heat for 3 minutes till the cheese melts. Serve piping hot.

Chapatti and Parantha

For those who eat wheat, *chapatti*, bread, *naan*, *parantha* and *tandoori roti* form the most essential element in their cuisine. A range of grains are used such as wheat, corn, millet, barley, *mandua*, chana and other lesser known ones. For those who are fasting, when no grains can be eaten, the flour of dried water chestnuts or *singhara* is used. In times of scarcity people use all kinds of ingredients for making chapatti. One of the most common substitutes is the inner kernel of the mango, normally discarded, which is dried and made into flour. A number of tubers are also used in different parts of the country to make flour. Besides the simple roti and chapatti, there are also the very exotic naan paneeri, *bhathura* and *katlama* made during Ramzan; from white flour. There is also the mughlai parantha, which is layered and is like an accordion, with one layer after another dripping in ghee. It is popular under different names, not only all over India, but wherever Indians have settled.

The *parat* for making dough, the griddle, the chapatti making stand or the *chakla* and the *belan* (the rolling pin), are essential kitchen implements in any North Indian household. Beautiful lacquered belans with silver *ghungroos* or bells at the ends were given as dowry. Brass or silver hollow belans contained little pebbles, which would make music as the bride rolled out chapattis.

The tandoor or *tanoor* as it is known in Central Asia was a part of life in the towns of the North West Frontier Province. Each locality had its *tandoorwala* who would make the roti for the different households. Women would send someone with the dough made into small balls and the tandoor man would flatten them into thick chapattis with both his hands, slap them to the sides of the tandoor and cook them. Often he would have a *dal*, which could be bought as well. This would save the women the chore of cooking.

We came to Delhi before the partition of the country and my mother had a tandoor on our roof. This was something special then and people would come expressly to eat tandoori roti and parantha.

With the partition and the advent of people from the North West Frontier, tandoori cuisine became popular. It is now seen as a part of the Indian cuisine. Indians are so adept at developing commercial ventures that today even tandoori nouvel cuisine is being marketed in New York.

Since I believe that food should be delicious, healthy and easy to cook, I do not advise people to eat any of the breads, naan and parantha made with white flour. For everyday food, I would recommend the use of wholewheat flour with the addition of bran.

In India we can still buy wheat, have it cleaned there and then, and milled. It is better to take the trouble to get freshly ground flour rather than to buy ready milled flour which is available off the shelf.

There are also the Khadi stores, the Gandhi Ashram, naturopathy and health stores, which give you organically grown wheat, and even porridge made from sprouted wheat and a range of special flours. A thing to remember is that ground flour if not stored properly can grow stale or get weevils very easily. One should keep flour in air-tight containers so that it can stay for more than two months, except during the rainy season.

Do get a special parat for kneading dough, as well as a griddle or *tawa*, with a handle. Of course you will get a chakla (round board to roll chapattis) and a *belan* and not have to use the cutting board and a milk bottle, as I used to do when living abroad.

How to Prepare Dough for Chapatti

The simplest of all things and yet the most complicated is to make a simple round chapatti which will puff up like a ball. Let me confess at the outset that I still cannot make them perfectly round. Therefore, I generally make the three cornered or square parantha or those that I can shape with my hands like tandoori roti, parantha, or makkai roti (corn bread).

Preparing the dough is very simple.

Put 2 cups wholewheat flour in a *parat* or a *thali* or in a round flat-bottomed plate with a rim. Slowly add water, approximately ½ to ¾ cup, and mix with your fingers until the flour sticks together. Begin making it into a ball and rolling it on the surface of the plate. Knead the flour for at least six to seven minutes and keep on one side of the parat. Cover with a damp cloth and set aside for at least one hour. It is now ready to be made into chapatti/roti, or parantha on the griddle as well as in the tandoor.

When preparing the chapatti, knead the dough once again with damp hands. Sprinkle ½ cup flour on a flat tray to use as you roll out the chapatti. Place the griddle, preferably one with a handle, on the fire to heat.

For dough made from 2 cups of flour, you can get approximately 15 to 18 chapattis. Make small balls the size of a mandarin orange by rolling the dough into the palm of your hand. Place them on a separate plate. If not using them immediately, cover with a damp cloth.

Take one ball and put it on the dry flour spread in the parat and press it down, flattening it. Do the same with the other side. Now sprinkle dry flour on the chakla and roll it out with an even pressure till it becomes 5" to 6" in diameter. As you roll, dip the chapatti into the dry flour so as to prevent it from sticking.

Place the rolled chapatti on a hot griddle. Within a few seconds, little bubbles will form on the surface. Turn with tongs (I use flat ice tongs). Cook the other side, and when they have brown spots, press down one side with a napkin rolled into a ball and rotate. The chapatti should puff up. Remove from the griddle. Serve it hot with a little butter or ghee on top, or put a little butter and keep covered, putting the chapattis one on top of the other, so that they remain soft.

Friends of mine who lived in New York used to make a

week's supply of chapatti and keep them in the freezer. They would take them out to defrost and then pop them into the toaster and eat them piping hot.

I also make dough in large quantity, wrap it in plastic and keep for a couple of days in the refrigerator, taking out the requisite amount when I need it.

PARANTHA SADA

Plain Parantha

- Prepare the dough as described on p. 289-291.

- Make into a chapatti.

- After it is rolled, spread oil or ghee thinly on half the side and fold over. Repeat the process and quarter the chapatti.

- Now pat it into the dry flour and roll it out as a three-cornered parantha.

- Put on the hot griddle and cook lightly on both sides until brown spots appear.

- Take ½ tsp ghee and rub it on the top of the parantha and turn. Do the same to the other side.

- Add ½ tsp ghee on the sides and fry on one side. Turn and do the same on the other.

- Eat hot and crisp.

SABZI WALA PARANTHA

Stuffed Parantha

There are two ways of making parantha with vegetables. One is to add the vegetables and spices to the dough, while the other is to place a layer in between two rolled, uncooked chapatti. The stuffed parantha is easier to make, more delicious and a meal in itself.

Chapatti and Parantha

ALU KA PARANTHA

Potato Parantha

Makes 4

2 medium-sized potatoes, boiled and mashed
1 green chilli, finely chopped (optional)
¾ tsp salt
¼ tsp dried pomegranate seeds, finely pounded
½ tsp dried mango powder (amchur)
½ cup oil or ghee

· Mix all together. Spread on the chapatti as described
on p. 292 and cook accordingly.

GOBI KA PARANTHA

Cauliflower Parantha

Makes 4

¾ cup grated cauliflower
½ tsp grated ginger
¾ tsp salt
1 green chilli, finely chopped
½ cup oil or ghee

· Mix all together. Spread as described on p. 292 and
cook accordingly.

PANEER KA PARANTHA

Cottage Cheese Parantha

Makes 4

½ cup cottage cheese (paneer), crushed or grated
1 onion, grated
1 green chilli, finely chopped
¼ tsp dried pomegranate seeds, crushed
½ tsp salt

· Mix all together. Spread on the chapatti as described on p. 292 and cook.

PUDINA PARANTHA
LACHEDAR

Layered Mint Parantha

Makes 8

1¼ cups wholewheat flour
1½ tsp dried mint, finely powdered
½ tsp salt
¼ tsp bishop's weed (ajwain)
½ cup oil or ghee

- To flour add 1 tsp mint, salt and ajwain and make into a dough as described on p. 289-291. Keep covered for two hours with a damp cloth.

- Roll into an oval chapatti with flour sprinkled on the rolling pin. Make it as thin and long as possible.

- Rub oil on half the side lengthways and fold over. Put oil on the folded area and tuck, pressing together. Repeat till the width is ½" to ¾". Lift and coil into a round in the palm of the hand.

- Press into flour and roll out into a circle.

- Cook in ghee as described on p. 292.

- Once it is ready, take off the griddle, sprinkle mint and rub in with a spoon.

- Serve with curd or cut into small pieces as a snack.

This can also be made without mint and is delicious either way.

KHAMEERI ROTI

Leavened Chapatti

Makes 6

1 cup wholewheat flour
½ tsp baking powder
½ tsp salt
¼ cup water

- Mix all the ingredients together, make into dough, wrap in a cloth and keep overnight in a warm place in winter and in a cool place in summer, but not in the refrigerator. The dough will rise.

- In the morning make 6 balls of dough.

- Clean the bottom of a griddle, place on the fire upside down and heat.

- Press ball of dough flat. Slap the dough from one hand to the other and make a thick circular chapatti.

- Slap it on the griddle and cook on both sides until the lightly raised bubbles turn brown.

- Spread a little butter on it and keep wrapped in a closed box.

Mother used to make khameeri roti for Grandmother on the ulta tawa, griddle turned upside down, so that she had the feeling that she was eating tandoori roti, as she did when in Abbotabad. The khameeri roti was also soft so she could eat it even without her dentures.

MAKKAI KI ROTI

Maize Flour Chapatti

Makes 4

1 cup maize flour
2 tbsp butter

· Put maize flour in a bowl and slowly add warm water, mixing the flour together. Roll into four parts and set aside.

· Moisten hands and place dough in the palm, press and rotate. If you have small hands, you can do it on the chakla by rotating the roti on a floured surface with the hand.

· Place on a hot griddle and cook on both sides until there are dark brown spots on them.

· Serve with melting butter.

MAKKAI KI ROTI WITH METHI

Fenugreek and Maize Chapatti

- Make dough as before, only add 2 tbsp chopped fenugreek or 1 tsp dry kasuri methi soaked for an hour, drained, squeezed and added to the flour.

MISSI ROTI

Chickpea Flour Chapatti

6 pieces

¾ cup chickpea flour (besan)
¼ cup wholewheat flour
½ tsp salt
1 onion, finely sliced
1 green chilli, finely chopped

- Mix the dry ingredients together first, then add onion and chilli. Add approximately ¼ cup water slowly and mix flour until it adheres together.

- Make into 6 balls and roll out or shape by hand into 6 thick chapatti.

- Cook on a hot griddle on both sides until brown. Serve with a dollop of ghee or butter.

For those who suffer from wheat allergy or diabetes, the missi roti can be prepared without wholewheat flour. The dough should be made into small-sized chapatti by hand.

TANDOORI ROTI

· You can improvise a tandoor out of a round tin 10" to 12" high and with a 10" diameter. Remove the covering from one side and clean the inside thoroughly, then put on the gas and heat the tin.

· Take one round ball of flour, the size of a small orange, and press it into the palm of the hand and flatten. Slap the roti with the palms until it is 5" in diameter.

· Turn the tin on its side over the fire and slap the roti on the inner side of the tin. Make a second roti and turn the tin around and slap it on the side. The tin can take 3 roti at a time.

· Turn the tin on the fire to cook the roti. When they are cooked, they will come off. You can roast them further on a low open gas flame, turning with a pair of tongs.

· Add ghee or butter.

TANDOORI PARANTHA

- Take a ball of dough and stretch it lengthwise. Put ghee on one side and fold over. Make a round of the dough and then by slapping between the two palms make it circular, approximately 5" in diameter. Cook in the improvised tin tandoor as described on p. 299.

KHAMEERI TANDOORI ROTI

- Prepare the flour as for Khameeri Roti (p. 296), only make it in the tandoor as a tandoori roti. It is soft and delicious.

TABBOULEH

Serves 6

1 cup burghul (cracked wheat)
½ cup chopped green coriander
¼ cup chopped mint
2 cucumbers
3 medium-sized tomatoes
Salt and pepper to taste
Juice of 2 limes
3 tbsp olive oil
¼ tsp chilli sauce
¼ cup chopped spring onion
1 onion, finely chopped
A few lettuce leaves

· Soak the burghul in 3 cups water and set aside for an hour or two. (I often use dalia instead of burghul.)

· Clean, destem and wash coriander and mint. Dry and chop them up and mix. Set aside.

· Drain the burghul and squeeze out the water. Mix with herbs.

· Peel cucumber, check for bitterness. If sweet, cut lengthwise into 8 portions and chop into bite-size pieces.

· Cut tomatoes into thin, long slices.

· Mix together salt, pepper, lime juice, olive oil, chilli sauce and mix with the burghul, herbs, tomatoes, onion and cucumber.

· Check taste and, if necessary, add more lime juice,

chilli sauce and salt, for burghul is very bland and the salad needs to be sharp and fragrant.

· Serve on a bed of lettuce leaves.

INDIAN TABBOULEH

Serves 6

The ingredients are the same as for Tabbouleh (p. 301), with the following additions:

2 tbsp oil
2 large onions, finely chopped
2 tsp cumin powder
½ tsp allspice
2 green chillies, finely chopped
3 tbsp tomato purée
1½ tsp chilli sauce
1½" ginger, finely sliced, soaked in lime juice
A few lettuce leaves

- Mix all the ingredients as described on p. 301.
- Put 2 tbsp oil in a frying pan and sauté the onions until golden. Add cumin powder, allspice and chillies and sauté for half a minute. Add tomato purée and sauté.
- Add the mixture to the burghul, along with chilli sauce and half the ginger soaked in lime juice. Mix all together.
- Refrigerate for at least 3 to 4 hours.
- Serve on a bed of lettuce leaves, sprinkling the remaining ginger on top.

303

BURGHUL PULAO

Serves 4

1½ cups burghul (cracked wheat)
3 cups water or vegetable stock
Salt and pepper to taste
4 tbsp butter or oil

· Rinse the burghul in water and sieve.

· In a heavy-bottomed pan with a lid put 3 cups water or vegetable stock. Add salt and pepper and bring to a boil. Add burghul and stir. Lower heat and simmer covered for 15 minutes until tender and till the water is absorbed.

· Stir in butter or oil.

· Put a napkin on the lid in case the pulao is damp, and cook for 5 minutes.

This is ideal for people who are allergic to rice. It can be made with the addition of fresh green chana, boiled or frozen peas, or boiled chickpeas. These should be added half way through the cooking.

Rice

Rice is an essential part of the diet in southern, eastern and western India. If the people in these places don't eat rice, they feel that they have not eaten. Boiled rice is the most common and best way of eating rice. The real rice eaters prefer it steamed and the most delicious way to eat it is hot and steaming with ghee and roasted dry chutneys, called *podi*, made in homes in Tamil Nadu and Andhra Pradesh. This is how one can begin a meal.

The Bengali way is to begin with *shukto*, which is bittersweet, followed with a thin yellow moong dal, fragrant with the leaves of the lime tree, *gandho raj*, the king of fragrance, put into the hot dal as it is taken off the fire.

In my experience, the most fragrant rice, which is even better than the finest basmati, is the *dum siah* from the

Caspian area in Iran. The aroma of the rice is heady and their way of eating beyond compare. The hot rice comes steaming to the table, its fragrance fills the air. It is ladled on to your plate with a pat of butter melting inside it. You quickly make a hole in the centre and add the yellow of a raw egg, sprinkle a bit of the sour red powder of *soumak,* and mix it all together and savour it. It is sheer bliss. Rice made in the Persian way with saffron, berries, *zarishk* and a crust can be eaten without any embellishment.

Here we have a few simple rice dishes for I find cookbooks never have recipes to tell you ways of making basic standard dishes. When I was learning to cook for my son in Addis Ababa, he wanted to eat khichri after a bout of illness. No cookbook told me how to make it. Finally, a resident Indian family came to my rescue after many jokes at the expense of inept working mothers!

BOILED RICE

Serves 4

1 cup long-grained rice
1 tsp salt

- Wash and drain rice.

- In a heavy-bottomed pan put 2½ cups water, bring to a boil, add the rice and salt and stir together.

- Cover tightly and cook for 25 minutes. Check the rice to see that it is soft and no grains remain. If not fully cooked, add ¼ cup boiling water. Keep lid on and finish cooking.

- Serve hot.

SABZI POLO

Herb Pulao

Serves 6

2 cups basmati rice
1 piece rock salt
1 cup chopped amaranth or spinach
¼ cup chopped green coriander
¼ cup finely chopped mint
½ cup spring onions, very finely cut
Salt to taste
4 tsp butter

- Wash and drain rice. Soak in 3 cups water with a lump of rock salt. If possible soak overnight, or for 4 to 6 hours.

- Drain and remove salt. In a heavy-bottomed pan with a lid, put 5 cups water, 1 tsp salt and bring to a boil.

- Add rice slowly. Boil vigorously for 4 minutes and add all the remaining ingredients except butter. Mix and continue to boil for another minute, or until the rice is soft with just a little grainy feel to it.

- Drain the rice in a colander or a sieve.

- Put 2 tbsp butter in a non-stick pan with lid. Put in the rice with a spoon. Add 2 tbsp butter on top. Wrap lid in a napkin, folding the ends over the top, and close tight. Put the rice on a very low flame and cook for 20 minutes. After 10 minutes place a griddle underneath the pot to reduce heat.

This is the Persian offering for the Nourouz lunch. Fried fish, another rarity, is served along with this. It heralds the coming of spring and traditionally the herbs should be fresh greens that emerge from the melting snow.

JOLLOF RICE

Serves 6

4 tbsp corn oil
250 gm onions, finely chopped
6 cloves garlic, finely chopped
750 gm tomatoes, skinned and chopped
Salt to taste
1 tsp black pepper
2 sticks cinnamon
2 cloves
2 bay leaves
1 tsp dried oregano (optional)
2 cups long-grained rice

- In a heavy-bottomed pan heat the oil and fry the onions until golden. Add garlic and sauté for half a minute.

- Add tomatoes, salt, pepper, cinnamon, cloves, bay leaves and oregano. Continue to fry for 5 minutes.

- Add 2 cups hot water and simmer for 10 minutes.

- Add the rice and stir well.

- Add 3 cups hot water and stir together.

- When the water boils, lower flame. Cover and cook for 20 minutes. You may put a griddle at the bottom for the last 5 minutes.

- Serve rice hot.

PERSIAN PULAO WITH TEHDEEG CRUST

2 cups long-grained basmati rice
2 tsp salt
½ cup butter
3 tbsp curd
3 tsp zarishk red berries, if available

- Wash rice thoroughly and soak in water with salt for 2 to 3 hours. Drain.

- Boil 6 to 7 cups water with 2 tsp salt. Add rice and boil for 15 to 20 minutes. Stir rice so that the grains don't stick together.

- Pour rice into a colander, drain and hold under tap to rinse cooked rice.

- In a teflon pan with a lid, put half the butter and ⅓ tbsp curd and cover the bottom of the pan and the sides.

- Take rice with a ladle and pour it into the pan to cover the bottom and let the remaining rice come up in a cone. Pour the remaining butter over it.

- Cook with lid for 10 minutes on a medium fire. In the last 3 minutes put a griddle underneath the pan.

- Cover lid with a napkin and fold it over the top. Close lid tightly. Cook on a low fire for 30 minutes.

- The rice will form a crisp and delicious crust at the bottom, which is known as Tehdeeg.

- Remove from fire and put pan in cold water which comes up to an inch or so from the bottom for 5 minutes.

- Turn the pot over in a large serving dish and it will come out like a cake. Serve immediately, garnished with berries.

The rice has to stay on the fire until ready to serve, otherwise it will get soft and lose its crispness.

ADAS PULAO

Masoor Dal and Rice

Serves 6

2 cups long-grained rice
½ cup Egyptian lentils (masoor dal)
Salt to taste
¼ cup sultanas
4 tbsp oil
2 sticks cinnamon
¼ tsp ground nutmeg
2 bay leaves
½ tsp black pepper
1 onion, finely chopped

· Clean and wash rice, drain and set aside.

· Clean, wash and drain dal. Put 5 cups water, 1 tsp salt and pressure cook for 10 minutes. Remove from fire, cool, open and drain. Reserve liquid and set dal aside.

· Soak sultanas in warm water and set aside.

· In a heavy-bottomed pan with a tight lid, heat 1 tbsp oil, add cinnamon, nutmeg, bay leaves and pepper and sauté for 1 minute.

· Fry the onion until golden. Add the rice and sauté for 1 minute. Add lentils and sauté for 1 minute. Now add sultanas and mix together.

· Add 2½ cups liquid from the lentils and if necessary supplement with water. Add salt. Stir everything.

315

Allow water to come to a boil, lower flame and simmer for 15 minutes. Check rice.

· Cover lid with a napkin and fold ends at the top before closing tightly. Simmer for 10 minutes at lowest possible temperature.

The *adas pulao* was considered the poor man's food and would never be offered to a guest. Claudia Roden gives the recipe known by its Arabic name, Megararra, which according to her was described 'by al-Baghdadi as a dish of the poor and (is) still known today as Easau's favourite'. My association with it is through a wonderful Namazi friend from Shiraz, who wailed in despair when I dropped in to see her at lunch time in Tehran, 'I have only *adas pilau*', which I ate with relish with fresh herbs and a *khoresht*.

KHICHRI SADI

Serves 4

1 cup rice
½ cup green gram (moong dal)
2 tbsp ghee
1 tsp cumin seeds
Salt to taste
½ tsp turmeric powder (optional)
6 cloves garlic, finely chopped

· Clean, wash and drain rice and dal. Mix together and set aside.

· In a heavy-bottomed pan heat 1 tbsp ghee.

· Add cumin seeds. When they are golden brown, add rice and dal and stir-fry for a minute on a low fire. Add 3 cups water, salt to taste, turmeric powder, and cover. Once the water boils, reduce flame and simmer for 20 minutes.

· As the khichri thickens, stir and if necessary place an iron/aluminium plate or griddle beneath to reduce heat.

· When the dal is cooked and soft, take off the fire and set aside, covered.

· Heat ghee in a small kadhai.

· Add garlic and fry until golden brown. Add to the khichri and mix.

· Serve hot.

This khichri is good for those who wish to avoid heavy or

rich food. If you have an upset stomach, avoid the tempering and add garlic while cooking at step one.

VEGETABLE KHICHURI

Serves 6

250 gm green gram (moong dal), washed and drained
250 gm rice, washed and drained
6 green cardamoms
250 gm cauliflower, separated into florets
100 gm shelled peas
200 gm potatoes, cut into quarters
100 gm small onions, peeled

For paste:

½ tsp coriander powder (optional)
½ tsp turmeric powder
2 tsp cumin powder
½ tsp chilli powder
1 tsp ginger paste

For tempering:

3 tbsp ghee
2 dry red chillies
2 tsp cumin seeds
1 tsp garam masala powder
6 green chillies, slit
2 bay leaves
2 onions, thinly sliced

· Measure the dal and rice mixture. Put double the
water into a heavy-bottomed pan. Bring the water to
a boil. Add rice, dal and cardamoms to the boiling
water and allow to cook till rice is half cooked.

· Grind together the ingredients for paste and stir it in.
Add salt to taste. Simmer for 5-7 minutes, mixing it
all together.

319

- Add the vegetables and continue to simmer till they are cooked (approximately 10 minutes). By this time, both rice and dal will be cooked as well.

- Heat the ghee in a frying pan. Sauté red chillies, spices and bay leaves for half a minute.

- Add sliced onions and fry till golden brown.

- Add to the cooked rice. Mix well, taking care not to crush the vegetables.

This is a meal in itself. You can serve it with fried aubergines, curd or by itself with butter.

The Bengalis make *khichuri* more like a vegetable pulao and it's a feast rather than the khichri which is meant for delicate stomachs. Traditionally, this dish is eaten on a rainy day. A Bengali housewife looks at the sky and decides the menu is *khichuri*, *bhaja* and *bhartha* with generous dollops of ghee. It is also a way of using what is available at home when the village roads could be flooded in a heavy downpour and markets cease to function. A combination of rice and dal which are always in stock at home, and whatever vegetables are growing in the garden, is a good stand-by.

JEERA PULAO

Cumin Rice

Serves 6

2 cups basmati rice
1 piece rock salt
2 tbsp oil
1 tsp cumin seeds
5 cardamoms
2 sticks cinnamon, 3" long
3 bay leaves
3 tsp butter
1 tsp salt

· Clean, wash and drain rice, then soak with rock salt for 2 hours.

· Heat oil in a heavy-bottomed pot (with tight-fitting lid) over medium heat, add the spices and stir for half a minute.

· Drain rice, take out salt, add rice to oil and fry, stirring, for a minute or two. Now put in 3½ cups water and salt. Bring to a boil, cover and reduce heat to low. Cook for 25 to 30 minutes, until done. Halfway through the cooking, stir gently with a fork. Make three holes in the rice and put in the butter.

· Put an aluminium plate or griddle under the pot to slow the cooking. Check rice by crushing one grain between your fingers. If the water has not yet evaporated, wrap lid of the pan in a napkin and put it back firmly.

CUMIN RICE WITH PEAS

Serves 4-6

- Get a 250 gm packet of frozen peas and add to the rice, cooked as in the earlier recipe, halfway through the cooking when the rice it still grainy. Cover and continue to cook.

LEFTOVER RICE WITH PEAS AND MUSHROOMS

Serves 4

4 tsp vegetable oil
½ tsp cumin seeds
1 medium-sized onion, peeled and finely chopped
6-8 medium-sized mushrooms, cleaned and chopped
½-1 fresh green chilli, finely sliced (optional)
250 gm frozen peas
2 cups plain leftover boiled rice
1 tsp salt

· Heat oil in a kadhai on medium flame. Add first the cumin, then the onions and fry until onions are transparent. Add mushrooms and fry for 1 minute, then add sliced green chilli, and after another minute, the frozen peas. Stir-fry for a minute.

· Finally add rice, breaking any lumps with a fork.

· Sprinkle water and stir-fry for 5 minutes.

· Put in 3 to 4 tbsp water with the salt mixed in it. Stir again.

· Cover, lower heat, and cook for 5 minutes. Place kadhai on a griddle to control heat. The rice must heat right through.

Serve hot.

MITHA CHAWAL

Sweet Rice

Serves 8

1½ cups long-grained rice
3 tbsp corn oil or ghee
2 sticks cinnamon
6 cloves
2 bay leaves
½ tsp peppercorn
1 tsp cumin seeds
2 tbsp sugar
3 tbsp brown sugar (shakkar)
½ cup sultanas, picked, washed and soaked in water for 30 min.
2 tbsp melted butter

- Clean, wash and drain rice. Soak in water for 2 hours.
- Heat oil or ghee in a large heavy-bottomed kadhai with a lid. Put in all the spices and stir for half a minute until the spices change colour.
- Add rice and stir-fry for 3 to 5 minutes.
- Add 2½ cups water, cover and cook for 8 to 12 minutes until rice is practically done.
- While the rice is cooking, put the sugar and brown sugar in ½ cup water and make into a syrup.
- Add syrup and sultanas to rice and stir them in. Cook covered for 5 minutes on a very low fire, preferably with a griddle underneath so as to lower heat. The rice by now should be cooked through.

- Remove lid and add melted butter. Stir-fry rice in the kadhai until the sides are crisp. Serve hot.

In the North West Frontier Province, from where I hail, sweet rice was an essential part of a festive meal, be it a wedding, a naming ceremony, or the birth of a son. We used to eat this with thinned curd or raita made with onions and green chillies, called *matha*. Part of the sweet rice would get burnt and that was a great favourite of the children. We used to fight over our share.

SHEER BERENJ
Rice Payasam/Rice Pudding

Serves 6

¼ cup broken rice
6 cardamoms, peeled and seeds powdered fine
1 stick cinnamon
3 cups milk
½ cup sultanas, picked, washed and soaked in water for 30 min.
⅓ cup sugar
1 tsp rose water
6 almonds, blanched and cut into slivers

- Clean, wash and drain rice. Soak in water for 1 hour and drain.

- Put rice with 1 cup water and all the spices and cook for 10 minutes in a heavy pot with lid. Add milk and cook, stirring for 20 minutes until rice is done and the milk has thickened.

- Add sultanas and sugar, stir together until the sugar is completely melted.

- This can be served hot in winter and cold in summer. If serving hot, take off the fire and add rose water. Pour into dish, remove spices and sprinkle almonds.

- If serving cold, cool, remove spices, mix rose water and half the almonds. Sprinkle the remaining almonds on top. Refrigerate overnight or at least for a couple of hours.

This is a common dessert and quite different from the rice

pudding of the English kitchen, the bane of children there. We loved this dessert and could never understand why the English and Anglo-Indian girls hated it, until I went to visit a cousin at boarding school. The North Indian word for this dish I never use—not after my sojourn in Iran, for there it means the phallic symbol.

The Sauce of
Life

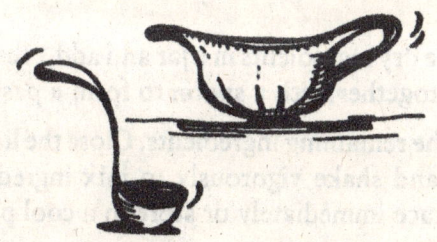

A judicious use of sauce can transform a dull meal into a feast. I always keep a few sauces in my refrigerator and some while travelling. I began doing this when my son was going to boarding school. He would carry with him sauces with which he could improvise a delectable snack with one minute noodles prepared on the forbidden stove, or add flavour to the chapattis and vegetables smuggled out of the dining room. In this section, I have given recipes for the basic sauces mentioned in the cookbook.

VINAIGRETTE SAUCE

Makes about ½ cup

⅓ tsp salt
¼ tsp black pepper
¼ tsp mustard seeds
5 tbsp olive oil, corn oil or sunflower oil
2 tbsp malt vinegar or lime juice

- Put the dry ingredients in a jar and add 1 tbsp oil. Mix them together with a spoon to form a paste.

- Add the remaining ingredients. Close the lid of the jar tight and shake vigorously to mix ingredients. Use the sauce immediately or store in a cool place.

CURD AND GARLIC DRESSING

Makes about ½ cup

½ cup low-fat curd
6 cloves garlic, made into paste
½ tsp salt
¼ tsp black pepper

· Beat the curd till smooth.

· In a bowl put garlic, salt and pepper and two tbsp curd. Mix together until it blends completely with the salt and pepper.

· Mix in the remaining curd and use immediately or refrigerate. Ideally, it should be used as soon as possible.

This is excellent low-fat dressing for green salads, boiled vegetables and salad.

BLENDER MAYONNAISE

Makes 1½ cups

1 egg
1 level tsp mustard powder
1 tsp salt
½ tsp black pepper
1 cup salad oil or corn oil
3 tbsp malt vinegar or lime juice

- Put egg, mustard, salt, pepper and ¼ cup oil in a blender and mix thoroughly.

- While running the blender at a slow speed, slowly add the remaining oil drop by drop. You will know from the sound of the blender that the sauce has thickened. If it does not thicken, add another egg. Then add oil in a thin stream slowly until all of it is absorbed.

- Add vinegar and mix.

- Refrigerate, but do not keep for more than 1 week.

HOME-MADE COTTAGE CHEESE

Makes ¾ cup

1 litre milk
1 tbsp lime juice

- Boil milk and add lime juice. When the milk curdles, remove from fire.

- In a colander put in a cheese cloth or thick mull cloth. Place colander over a pan and pour in the curdled milk. Allow the whey to drain completely. Tie the cloth together and hang it for half an hour from the faucet in the sink.

- Remove cottage cheese (paneer) from the cloth. It can be used immediately or refrigerated.

The drained whey is an excellent cooling drink and easy to digest. In fact, in the Ayurvedic system, people suffering from acute digestive problems are told to drink whey as a means of nutrition. It can be prepared like buttermilk with a little rock salt and ground cumin powder, or with brown sugar.

COTTAGE CHEESE SAUCE

Makes approx. ½ cup

½ cup home-made cottage cheese (paneer)
1 tbsp chopped coriander
2 tbsp curd
Salt and pepper to taste

- Mash paneer coarsely.

- Mix everything together.

- Use immediately.

INDIAN PESTO SAUCE

Makes 1 cup

1½ cups basil
6 cloves garlic
¼ cup peanuts or cashew nuts, freshly roasted
4 tbsp olive oil or sunflower oil
2 tbsp lime juice
1 level tsp salt
½ tsp black pepper
½ cup Parmesan

- Clean basil and chop fine. Crush garlic.
- Put all the ingredients in a blender and purée together.
- Refrigerate.

This is a multi-purpose sauce which can be mixed with pasta or used as a sandwich spread. It can be put on wholewheat chapatti or toasted brown bread. I also use it as a marinade for fish fillet grilled in an oven.

DRY CHILLI AND GARLIC SAUCE

Makes ½ cup

10 dry red chillies
10 cloves garlic
2 tbsp olive oil or corn oil or Saffola
1 tsp salt

- Deseed the dried chillies and discard the seeds. Pound the chilli skins into tiny flakes.

- Chop garlic very fine and sauté in oil until fragrant.

- Add chilli and salt and stir-fry for half a minute, mixing well.

- Place in a bottle when cool and close lid tightly.

This is the traditional Italian *aglio olio e peperoncino* sauce, which I learned from my friend, Paoula. The sauce can be kept in a semi-dry state and mixed with olive oil or salad oil when needed for pasta or boiled vegetables.

TOMATO SAUCE

Makes 2 cups

2 tbsp oil
1 onion, finely chopped
6 cloves garlic, very finely chopped
¼ tsp chilli powder
½ tsp cumin powder
½ tsp black pepper
1 tsp salt
500 gm tomatoes, skinned, chopped and pureed

· Heat oil and sauté onion and garlic until transparent

· Add spices and sauté for half a minute.

· Add tomato and cook for 10 to 15 minutes until thickens.

· Keep refrigerated in a jar.

NAM PRIK

My version of the Thai sauce for non-conservative vegetarians:

Makes 1 cup

1 tbsp tamarind, soaked in 2 tbsp vinegar
7 dry red chillies
2 tbsp vinegar
1 tbsp soya sauce
2 tbsp nam pla
3 tsp salt
1 tsp jaggery
3 tbsp sunflower oil

· Make a paste of the tamarind and set aside.
· Pound the dry red chillies and mix with tamarind paste and vinegar.
· Mix all the ingredients and purée in a blender.
· Spoon into a jar and seal tightly.

This is rather a strong sauce which can be used as a marinade and even in soups and noodles, for it has the exotic flavour of Thai cuisine.

Simple Desserts

INSTANT BANANA AND ORANGE DESSERT

Serves 6

2 tbsp butter
5 ripe bananas
Juice of 2 oranges
Juice of 1 lime
2 tbsp honey
2 tbsp brandy

· In a frying pan melt butter.

· Peel bananas. Cut lengthwise into pieces, add to butter.

· Stir-fry for 1 minute.

· Add lime juice and orange juice and stir.

· Add honey on top and stir.

· Take off fire. Add brandy and serve hot.

MANGO DELIGHT-I

Serves 6

300 gm aam papad (dried sheets of mango juice), light coloured
½ litre milk
4 tbsp sugar
4 drops vanilla essence
1 tbsp pistachio slivers (optional)

- Soak aam papad in milk with sugar in refrigerator overnight.

- Put all ingredients except pistachio in a blender and mix together.

- Pour into serving dish. Sprinkle pistachio on top and refrigerate for at least an hour before serving.

MANGO DELIGHT-II

Serves 6

1 kg sweet mangoes
½ litre milk
3 drops vanilla essence

- Skin and cut mangoes.
- Reserve 2 cups of neatly cut mango pieces and set aside.
- Blend mangoes, milk and vanilla essence.
- In a shallow dish arrange mango pieces around the rim and pour in the mixture.
- Refrigerate for at least an hour before serving.

APRICOT DELIGHT

Serves 6

1 cup dried apricots, deseeded
¾ litre milk
4 tbsp sugar
4 drops vanilla essence
1 tsp almond slivers

- Chop dried apricots and soak in milk with sugar overnight.
- Add vanilla essence and mix in a blender.
- Pour into serving dish. Sprinkle almonds and refrigerate.

FIG DESSERT-I

Serves 6

200 gm dried figs
2 tbsp sugar
½ litre milk
4 drops vanilla essence

· Soak figs for one hour in warm water and rub them clean. Discard water.

· Chop figs and cook in ½ cup water and sugar for 10 minutes. Remove and cool.

· Mix figs and milk in a blender, then add vanilla essence.

· Pour into serving dish and refrigerate.

FIG DESSERT-II

Serves 6

500 gm figs
1 stick cinnamon
10 cardamoms
3 tbsp sugar
200 gm cream

- Soak figs (as for Fig Dessert-I, p. 347).

- Cut figs into 4 pieces.

- Put 2 cups water to boil.

- Add cinnamon, cardamom, figs and sugar and cook for 15 minutes until figs are soft. Remove from fire and cool.

- Serve at room temperature with cream.

PETHA PAYASAM

Ash Gourd Dessert

Serves 6

1 litre milk
500 gm petha (ash gourd), skinned and grated
4 tbsp sugar
6 green cardamoms

- Boil milk with grated petha and sugar, stirring frequently for 5 minutes. Lower heat and allow to simmer for 20 minutes until reduced to half the quantity. Keep stirring from the side and the bottom.

- Peel the cardamoms and powder the seeds, then add to the payasam and stir. Pour into serving bowl. Can be served hot or cold.

- Gaajar Payasam and Ghia Payasam can be made in the same manner.

GOLDEN PAYASAM

Serves 6

500 gm carrots
¾ litre milk
3 tbsp sugar or 4 tbsp shakkar (powdered brown sugar)
4 cardamoms with seeds, powdered
6 almonds, blanched and cut into slivers

· Grate carrots and set aside.

· Put milk in a pan on a slow fire and add carrots, sugar and cardamom and simmer, stirring constantly until the milk thickens. It will take 20 to 30 minutes depending on the quality of milk.

· In winter you can serve the dish hot with a sprinkling of almonds. In summer serve chilled.

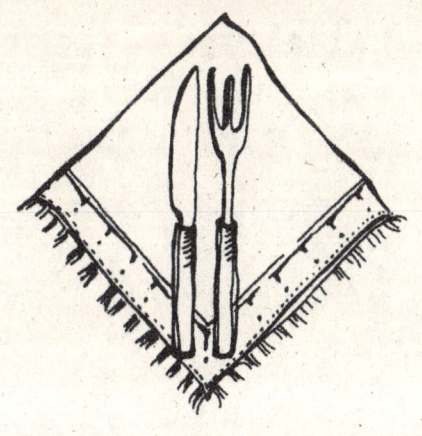

Finer Points of Cooking

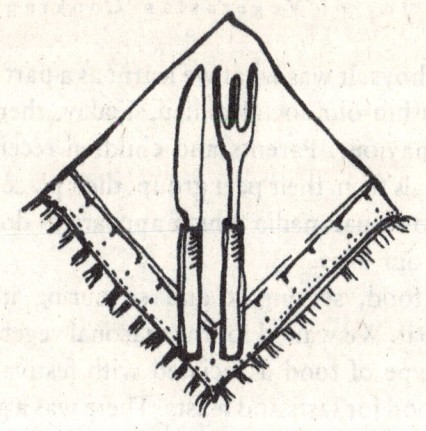

the etiquette
of cooking,
serving and
eating

There is a proper way of doing everything. I remember
in my home we were all taught how to sit. We had to
learn to sit sideways with our legs tucked beneath us, and
when we sat on a low chair, we had to do so without
pointing our feet towards a person or a revered object. We
were similarly taught how to eat in a proper manner and
how to serve others and ourselves. We even had to learn
how to accept a gift and how to offer one. This was not like
an authoritarian training reserved only for girls, it was also

taught to the boys. It was what we learnt as a part of day to day living within our social milieu. Today, there are no norms of behaviour. Parents and children receive many different signals from their peer group, their place of work, and the audio-visual media which appears to dominate a good part of our lives.

Cooking food, serving it and savouring it had an excitement to it. We waited for the seasonal vegetables, we cooked the type of food associated with festivals. There was special food for fasts and feasts. There was a great deal of anticipation involved in these activities.

In a Gujarati household, Makar-Sankranti—the winter equinox—was always celebrated on 14 January. It was the day for flying kites and eating the delicious mixed vegetable *oundhia* cooked in a clay pot, its preparation involving the entire family. The combination sesame seeds and jaggery was another delicacy that was seasonal. The dal cooked in thickened sugarcane juice was another. Of course, for the Punjabis the mustard greens, *sarason ka saga*, as we used to call it, cooked on a slow fire and eaten with cornflour bread, *makkai di roti*, remains a great favourite. So also the hot, crisply fried *pakoras* on a rainy day, or the *purra,* pancakes made from a batter of flour, jaggery and aniseeds which we would eat with cream from the top of the milk.

Cooking, sharing and feasting followed each season. If the summer came early and the devilishly hot winds blew mercilessly, we would console ourselves with the hope that the mangoes would be very sweet. Now cooking has become a chore and these celebrations long forgotten. Cold storage and easy transportation provide us with off-season vegetables and fruits which have made us very blasé.

However, we have also become more adventurous and are willing to try all kinds of fruit and food. Dried *sounth* or ginger, and dried thyme can be found in the same shelf. The dried *leemu Ommani* and walnuts can be found in the same kitchen. *Aam papad,* dried sheets of mango juice, sheets of apricot juice and *ab-nararang*, orange flower water, and *gulabarak,* rose water, are all easily available.

There are certain practical steps to cooking and it becomes much easier if we have the right cooking vessels, stirrers, colanders and the ingredients well arranged. It is a good idea for all new cooks to decide on the menu, prepare the ingredients and keep them in readiness before beginning to cook. Clean used vessels as you proceed with the cooking so that you do not have a stack of oily dishes to wash later.

There is an art to cutting and preparing vegetables. When I first arrived in Ahmedabad, I was quite amazed at how a little bit of vegetable was made to feed a large number of people. My friends would cut one small green mango into thin slices, retaining the dark green outer skin in each slice and then sprinkle it with a little salt and juice of lime and admire the colours. The Jain families who strictly observe 'ahimsa'—non-violence—would open the beans so as to allow any insects trapped inside to escape, and then chop the beans fine. The cooked vegetable would then become a subtle combination of two greens. The leaves of a cabbage were also opened before cutting and each flower of the cauliflower would be separated before being slit into tiny florets. Six years of my stay made me appreciate their subtle, austere and aesthetic ways. I remember walking into Kumudini Lakhia's home and seeing a large bottle of pickle on her marble table top, with huge pieces of cauliflower and beet standing rather aggressively in the bottle. I called out: Kumi, where did you get this obscene pickle? Her prompt reply was: From your part of the world!

I must say though, that my Gujarati friends did enjoy the food at my house for its variation and attention to different flavours and possibly a certain opulence, in cooking, flavouring and presentation, which is part of my north Indian culture and upbringing.

We, in India, have a varied and rich tradition of serving food. Normally, people are served food and do not help themselves. In a traditional Bengali kitchen, the meal starts with bitter vegetable, which is eaten with a little bit of rice and ghee. The bitter taste is supposed to secrete the digestive juices in the body to enhance one's appetite. This is followed by yellow dal, mildly sweetened and made fragrant with the addition of the leaves of the scented lime plant *gandharaj*. A bit of fried vegetable or bhaja is served with this. Next the delicately spiced vegetables and the *mach bhaja*, crisply fried fish. Meat or chicken comes next. With each course the food becomes more spicy. The *bhapa Ilish* or hilsa steamed and spiced with mustard and poppy seeds is a great delicacy. The meal ends with *touk*, sour-sweet unripe mango chutney or tomato chutney, to clear the palate and help digest the meal. Traditionally, the lady of the house serves and observes the guests to see which dish is relished the most and this would be served a second time. Other specialities of Bengali cuisine are the sweets made with fresh cottage cheese, the *shandesh*, the *rasmalai*, the *rasagolla*. This is possibly because of the Portuguese influence, for the Aryan dietary regulations are against the curdling of milk. The Portuguese, who had settled in Bengal in the seventeenth century, used to make cheese by curdling milk.

Gujaratis also have a very refined way of serving food with a balance of tastes, flavours and aromas and an infinite variety of dishes, savouries and pickles.

Sweet rice is a festive food for all non-rice eaters. I remember that on feast days or weddings we used to get sweet rice served with a salty raita of thin curd mixed with onions and cucumbers or with *bundi*, fried drop dumplings.

The big feasts held during marriages, ancestral worship ceremonies or death ceremonies are served in a traditional manner where the menu is based on the customs of the community and the method of serving is also prescribed. The top end of the banana leaf is kept to the right hand of the person being served. The fresh green top of the leaf faces the invitee and he is offered water to sprinkle and cleanse the leaf. The vein of the banana leaf divides the leaf into two sections. The section nearest is where the rice, puris and the main meal such as the curries are served, while the upper leaf is for the flavours, salt, chutney, salads, dried vegetables, and savouries.

Manipuris have the most elegant way of serving. I was once invited to a feast for the local deity, Lord Vishnu. The platter was made from a banana leaf cut into a perfect oval and boat-shaped banana containers were placed in front for the sauces. The meal was entirely vegetarian. Brahmin cooks dressed in white with a cloth tied round their nose and mouth, so as not to inhale the aroma of the food, served first the Gods and then us. For, even inhaling the aroma could pollute the food and it could not then be offered to the gods or the guests. Delicate vegetable curries, dals and fried vegetables were served to us. Tendrils of peas were made into a salad almost like delicate filigreed patterns, picked up by tiny golden globules of the dry chutney sprinkled on it, which looked and tasted good. Dals lightly seasoned with a range of flavouring, the most delicate being the one cooked with pineapple, were served piping hot. I counted twenty-six dishes and the hosts kept apologizing that this was a poor meal. I asked naively: if this is a poor meal, what would be the full service, and the incredible reply was, 101 dishes at least.

A delicate child sitting next to me had her *phanek*-clad legs tucked to her side and she ate with the tips of her fingers, not letting a drop fall out of her platter. Her fingers were clean and the food never went above the first joints of her fingers. I was enchanted by her exquisite manners and felt like a bear sitting next to her, trying to make my limbs obey me and not go into contortions and my hand to carry the delicious curries to my mouth without spraying everyone around me! We finished the meal with a sour, sweet dish of lemons in syrup which acted like an instant digestive.

Today, the etiquette has changed. The left hand, which was never used for serving or for eating and drinking as it was used for cleansing below the waist, is now used for serving ourselves or others, for the right is polluted by the act of eating with our fingers. The glass of water is also kept on the left hand, so that it does not carry the marks of food and appear unseemly on the table. People are horrified if guests help themselves with the right hand, whereas a couple of decades ago they would have been insulted if someone had served themselves or others with the left hand.

I remember that when I travelled abroad and stayed

with European friends I found it impossible to eat if they pushed their fork into the serving dish and picked up their favourite pieces. The practice was nauseating for me and it required a lot of self-discipline to accept it. Even today I look away when I see people indulging in this uncouth habit.

A lot of cooks in the West taste from the ladle while cooking. It may once have been sophisticated to do so but today even in the West they do not think it is a healthy practice. I consider it really bad manners and lack of consideration for others. The old concept of pollution is not old hat but is a sensible way of keeping one's viruses to oneself. The concept of *jutha* or pollution is not only connected with casteism, but also with hygiene. Research in the West has shown that one can imbibe thousands of microbes while sharing ice creams or eating from the same spoon.

We have to teach ourselves and our children to respect traditions and also the changes that are taking place, and to follow those norms which are acceptable. Sensitivity to others, to the overall atmosphere and an openness in approach, point the way to proper norms of behaviour.

vessels for cooking and for eating

The Sanskrit word for vessels, *patram*, means 'made of leaves'. Perhaps the original containers were made from leaves, in the days when we were food gatherers and shaped containers from leaves so as to carry more than what the cupped hand could hold. In fact, there are some very strict sects of sanyasis, who are known as *karpattar*, who do not use vessels. The Digambara, sky-clad Jain sanyasis, ate only once and that too what was poured into their cupped hands. They saw the *patram* as a way of being enslaved by *Maya*, or the illusory world.

In fact the association of the word *patr*, as a container,

has many connotations. It is applied to the actor who becomes a container for the role that he enacts. It is applied even to the bridegroom who takes over the responsibility of the protection of the bride. Of course, feminists do not approve of that concept for we presume, naturally, that woman contains man!

Thus vessels are shaped to contain, preserve, simmer, steam, fry and bake. In the traditional Indian context, the very act of preparation is an act of worship, for it is a form of *bhog*, a culmination of the act of creation, a ritual offering to the gods and then to those who share the food made for the gods by the Lakshmi of the house. As a child, I remember when my grandmother made chapatti, the first two were kept to be offered to God, who was represented by any passing mendicant or a needy person. My mother-in-law, who ate only two chapattis at lunch, would set aside half a chapatti to feed the sparrows. When I protested and said, why don't you eat your two chapattis and take one from the kitchen, she replied gently: I earn merit if I share what I need.

Earlier, only women used to cook, but now a number of men take great pleasure in cooking. In fact, the finest cooks among my younger friends are men. Daniel, who spent his childhood in India and his teenage years in Iran and now lives in Rome, is a superb cook. He not only uses traditional ingredients, but also traditional vessels. It is amusing to walk into his apartment in a fashionable quarter in Rome, to find virgin olive oil on the same kitchen shelf as gingelly oil, that too hand-pressed in India. Himman, my son, has also learnt to improvise and turns out a wonderful meal with an odd assortment of herbs, blending European and Indian flavours and turning out a delicately flavoured dish for his wife, since she has an extremely sensitive digestive system. He is very protective of his instruments. Don't touch my pan. Please leave my stirrer alone! Mamma, don't wash the dishes. I will have to do them again, is the refrain I hear when I visit him in Sydney.

India is a vast country with a range of cuisines which vary not only on a regional basis but also from one area to another. For instance, Gujarat has not just one cuisine, but innumerable variations which are quite distinctive. The best food is Surati food which the Gujaratis compare to the finest cuisines: *Banaras ka maran, Surat ka jaman*. Kaithiawaris have their own cuisine and so do the Ahmedabadis. What I love for its flavour and also for maintaining the miserliness associated with the Ahmedabadis is the *fajaido*, which means counterfeit. It is a thin sauce made from leftover curd clinging to the bottom of a mud dish, washed out with water, boiled with the seeds of mangoes from which the juice has been extracted, thickened with a spoon of *besan*, the flour of black gram, and delicately tempered with spices. It is a subtle dish made from practically nothing.

In the desert areas of Saurashtra when vegetables are difficult to come by and even the dried *ker*, the fruit of the desert, is not available, the women cheat the palate by collecting tiny rounded smooth stones the size of large white chickpeas and immersing them in a melange of spices prepared for pickle. The stone is sucked to simulate the effect of the *ker* seeds.

Every area also has traditional shapes and materials from which vessels for cooking and serving are made. In northern India, the Hindus cooked in brass vessels which were silvered inside, while Muslims cooked in silvered copper vessels. Copper vessels are used by the Hindus for worship. Earlier, while the affluent ate out of silver vessels, the well-to-do used bell-metal utensils. Those at the lower economic scale ate out of tinned brass bowls while the poor had to make do with leaves. In the case of the Tamil Brahmins only silver was considered pure and they either ate in silver vessels or on banana leaves. The Muslims ate out of large communal round trays or plates.

The vessel commonly used throughout India for cooking is the *kadhai*, a wok with heavy handles, which could be of varying sizes, from very small to extremely large ones for use during feasts. These could be of brass, copper or iron and are used for stir-frying vegetables that do not need protracted cooking. The iron kadhai is used for frying fish and vegetables, which are not curried and do not contain sour ingredients. The kadhai is also used for deep-frying. The shallow flat silvered kadhai is used by milk sellers and sweetmeat makers for thickening milk for *rabri* and *payasam*. In Kerala, one of the most beautiful vessels is the *warpa* or *urlie* made of bell metal which is used for making sweet payasam. Its sculpted shape balanced by the handle which, shaped like the curved horns of a ram, is a delight to the eye. It is a common sight even today when you visit a temple in Kerala to see a number of burnished urlie drying in the sun.

The handi is shaped like a lota, except it is squatter, has a wider mouth and a rounded base. It was used for cooking lentils and those dishes which have a great deal of thin sauce and take a long time to cook or need to be simmered. The curved bottom distributes the heat and the narrow neck contains it. The pan-like *patila* or *degchi* is deep, open-mouthed and with a rounded bottom which is broader than the top. It is used for roasting spices and meat or vegetables and has a lid that can be closed tightly. It is also used for giving *dum*, cooking in its own steam. This is done by sealing the lid with flour and also by putting pieces of coal on top of the lid, so that it cooks on slow heat from the top and bottom. Today, the cuisine *dumpukht* has become famous for delicate aromas.

The small iron kadhai or the long-handled iron bowl used for tempering (*tarka*), is an essential item of the Indian kitchen. Oil or ghee is heated along with the spices until it sizzles and then the entire bowl is plunged into the degchi and the sizzling tarka, combined with the taste of heated iron, adds an extra zing to the dal.

The griddle or *tawa* is also made of thick iron and is perfect for making chapatti, parantha and for roasting spices. It is also ideal for making cutlets and vegetables with minimal use of oil, just enough to make them crisp.

Generally, people sit in the kitchen and are served straight from the cooking vessels rather than from separate serving dishes. I remember a delicious Kashmiri *wasavan* feast prepared for me and my guests by my friend Madhhposh, who was a specialist in copper ware. He served us himself and each item of the meal was brought out in a beautifully shaped copper handi wrapped in a white cloth, and he explained the dish as he served us. My seventy-year-old guest, Salim Shallon, who was on his honeymoon in Srinagar, felt the only irritant in his paradise was the awful English food served to him and his wife by the owners of the houseboat, Lady of Shallot: Hot & Cold (they meant the plumbing). He could not understand how people renowned for their delectable cuisine, served with such sophistication, could dish out what was being offered to them everyday.

In Tamil Nadu, they not only have distinct vessels for cooking different food, but the vessels are also made of different material. The *chembu* or lota-shaped rasam pot is made from a special black alloy called *eyem* and the rasam made in it tastes very different. The favourite sambar pot is made of stone and is known as *kalachatti* and the wok is the *banvi*, which is made of iron. The idli *patram* is beautifully shaped and ideal for steaming. Traditionally, people ate on banana leaves and when fresh leaves were not available, dry banana leaves were brought out and spread for serving the meal. The use of metal plates came in later and china plates are indeed a very recent phenomenon, since earlier they were considered impure. Traditionally, Hindus would use unglazed clay pots only once and then discard them.

Today, we have the choice of a range of traditional vessels to cook in, to serve and to eat from. Bengal has begun to make light bell metal plates for everyday use, and beautifully shaped bowls and glasses are also available for serving a traditional meal.

The bell metal urlie and warpa, shallow and broad mouthed, make beautiful serving dishes. Brass parat for making dough, now available in small sizes, is ideal for serving rice. The *battie*, half-spherical bell-metal bowl, used by the people of Saurashtra for eating food, is another excellent serving dish. Orissa too has a range of bell-metal vessels, from the ones used for haldi and gram flour for the baby's massage, to the containers for dal and vegetable, which make elegant serving dishes. You can cook in them and bring them straight to the table. Soft stone bowls, available in a range of muted colours, are exquisite dishes for serving soups, yoghurt and desserts.

The Jain sadhus use lathe turned light wooden bowls to serve and eat from. An extraordinary large salad bowl can be improvised from the wooden container shaped like a tortoise and made from a single piece of wood, carried by fishmongers in the West Coast. I came across them in use amongst the women selling fish in Daman.

Today, the range of crockery is limitless. My favourite tableware consists of wooden plates with stone soup bowls, steel cutlery and bell-metal serving dishes. For a traditional Indian meal, I love to use bell-metal thalis and glasses, bell-metal bowls from Bengal and serving dishes of bell metal from Kerala such as the urlie, the warpa. The handi shaped bell metal from Orissa is great for curried dishes while the parat is excellent for serving pulao. I like to serve curd in a stone bowl from Gaya, while the chapattis are served wrapped in a napkin and kept in a sikki grass basket from Mithila, lovingly made by the sister of Jaffar, our electrician, who comes from that area.

Chotelalji, my bright young cook, has *rasa* in his hand. He loves to experiment in the kitchen along with me. He also tends to go off on his own cooking trip and I have a difficult time trying to make him follow my recipes. He loves not only to cook but also to serve people and takes great pride in doing so elegantly. The only thing is that he does not approve of my love for wooden plates, which he has finally succeeded in tucking away out of my reach. My sister, a cook par excellence, has been part of this sabotage for she always felt the wooden plates were infra dig.

basic dietary guidance for different conditions

The traditional Indian diets were moderate, balanced and far from self-indulgent. They relied mostly on the intake of cereals with leafy vegetables, milk, curd, pulses, fruits and a range of condiments. People ate seasonal vegetables and fruits and those that were locally grown. These were products of the local geo-climatic conditions and therefore the most suitable. Today, fruits and vegetables are available all year round, and different food brought in from different areas, thus our dietary habits are no longer in consonance with the climate or the diurnal rhythms of changing seasons.

When we were young we were told that summer produced vegetables and fruits which were a protection against the weather. The blistering heat of summer, combined with the searingly hot winds, were indications that the mangoes would be sweet and plentiful. The song of the nightingale, or koel, from the mango orchards as it feverishly called out while flitting from one bunch of mango blossoms to another, was further confirmation. The unripe mango sherbet, *panna*, made from roasted or boiled green mangoes by crushing them in cold water with brown sugar, is the best antidote for heat stroke. The green vegetables such as bottle gourd and members of the squash family are also cooling and soothing. Melons and cucumbers grown on the hot burning sands of the dry river beds are the sweetest. As a child living in Khyber Pass in the old Civil Lines area, a summer outing entailed a walk to Majnu-ka-Tila for the purchase of watermelons, which were set to cool in the waters while we swam. After our swim, we would feast on the cool melon and return home satiated. Mother would immediately serve us chilled homemade sherbet, for drinking sherbet after eating melons is essential. Similarly, *kachi lassi*, thinned sweet milk, must be taken after a feast of mangoes. The best way to know what is seasonal, no matter where you live, is by finding out which vegetables are the cheapest. These will not only be seasonal but also fresh, for they will be locally grown.

In Bengal, the eating of bitter vegetables to start the meal not only improves one's appetite but also purifies the blood and prevents stomach disorders. Dr Ishwar Sharma feels that the basic rule to follow is to try to eat the fruits and vegetables of the area where one is living, when these are in season. He also advises that one should learn about the traditional food combinations and as far as possible abide by them.

In India, our main intake of food comprises carbohydrates, mainly cereals, along with a small quantity of protein in the form of lentils and vegetables, dairy products and spices. Fruits are eaten traditionally in season and, typically, do not follow a meal but are eaten separately.

A simple, non-westernized north Indian's daily meal in an urban and rural context would be:

Breakfast of tea or a glass of milk or buttermilk, with leftover chapattis of the previous night.

Lunch would be again chapattis and/or rice with a ladle of thin pureed lentils, ½ cup home-made curd, a ladle of vegetables and pickles along with a little jaggery.

The evening meal would be a repeat of the same food as lunch, but possibly without curd.

In south India many households have rice for all three meals.

In the morning kunjee and/or leftover rice with pickles or leftover vegetables would be eaten.

Sufficient quantities of rice would be prepared for the afternoon and also for the evening. A seasonal curried vegetable or sambar made from a small quantity of lentils, just a handful, for a family of six, would be cooked with a large quantity of water and spices. The rice would be served with ghee and there would be pickles accompanying the rice. The meal would end with rice and curd or buttermilk and pickles.

The main objective is to eat enough cereals. In the case of chapattis, a spicy accompaniment in the form of a chutney, ground chillies and salt is eaten and in the case of rice, a thin, spicy soup-like dish is what is normally taken.

Large consumption of vegetables, lentils and curd was never a part of the Indian eating tradition. When I went to stay in Ahmedabad, I would see my well-to-do neighbours cooking 50 gm lentils and 100 gm vegetables for a family of ten persons. The round thali would be served with little bowls of dal, thinned curd, a spoon of vegetables, a spoon of chopped salad, a piece of pickle, a wedge of lime, a piece of jaggery and roasted papad. Rice would follow the chapatti. Fruits were a part of the meal. Cooked guava or papaya often replaced the vegetable. Mangoes would be juiced, cooked or pickled. Only seasonal fruits and vegetables would be used. This was regulated by fixing special days for starting to eat a particular vegetable or fruit. Every family would, during the season, have large quantities of a certain fruit, when they would get a basket from their garden or when the fruit was available at throwaway prices, or even during fasts when cereals were forbidden.

Most households did not eat meat or fish, for often the older generation would be vegetarian. The younger men would sometimes cook meat for special occasions. Of course, the Bengalis, Oriyas and the coastal people throughout India eat fish. Amongst Muslims, the eating of meat is essential, but not always affordable. So a large dish of vegetables would contain 100 gm meat, which would flavour the food. The head of the family and the male members would be given the meat pieces.

It was only in affluent homes that fresh food was

cooked for each meal and a range of dishes provided. I remember, in my home, food was cooked for each meal, but what we ate was very simple. For breakfast, paranthas were eaten with tea by the adults or with a glass of milk in the case of children. Lunch consisted of dal, vegetable, curd and chapatti. Tea was a simple cup of tea or a glass of milk for the kids with some home-made savouries and dinner was more or less a repeat of the morning, but without curd.

Meat was cooked once a month or when there were guests. Dessert was also cooked on occasion. There were, however, seasonal specialities and fruit was also eaten during the season; the latter often replaced a meal.

Traditionally, everyone fasted at least on one particular day of the week. In addition, there were the fasts associated with the phases of the moon, which were generally kept by women. Pooranmashi, the full moon, was a day of fasting that ended with saltless food. Amavas, the dark night, was a complete fast. During Ekadasi, the eleventh day of the Shukl Paksh, the fifteen days of moonlight, and the eleventh day of Krishna Paksh, the fifteen days of darkness, meals were taken once a day. Another period of fasting was the Navaratras, the nine nights devoted to the mother goddess, every six months, when no cereals were eaten. These were the days of *phalahar*, fruit eating.

Women also kept seventy-two vratas, fasts, which had different associations: for the long life of their husbands, for finding a good husband and then hanging on to him, for the well-being of their children, for the ancestors and for the *nakshatras*, the planets, that rule their lives. While researching on fasts, I came across another interesting fact; that sexual intercourse was also ruled by fasts and festivals and phases of the moon. If combined with menstruation and family rituals of birth and death anniversaries, the days of prohibition far exceeded the days on which a man and woman could be together.

Shivratri and Janamashtami were important festivals when everyone fasted. Cereals were not consumed but people feasted on sweets, fruits and other delicacies. It was what the children loved, for they could indulge themselves on forbidden goodies to their heart's content, once the fast was broken.

Fasting sometimes had another purpose. The well-to-do fasted and fed the Brahmins as well as those who were deprived. *Nirjalekadasi*, which came at the height of summer, was a fast when no water was drunk. But people set up little kiosks at the crossroads, offering cool sherbet to all the passers-by. In addition, they offered baskets of mangoes, melons and seasonal fruits to the poor sections of the community so that they too could feast.

Amongst the Muslims and Christians, of course, there was the extended period of fasting during Ramzan and Lent and it cut across gender and age.

It is interesting that on an average, Hindu men kept at least sixty days of fast, while the women kept twice as many. During these fasts, while the digestive system was given a rest, the intake of fruits and a saltless diet helped cleanse the system.

If we examine the food intake of the average Indian family, it is basically a healthy diet. The combination of a ladle of light dal with a ladle of a raita or matha, that is curd with the butter extracted, is not harmful. Problems arose when we began consuming Indian food in the western style by eating large quantities of meat, dal, curd and very little vegetable, fruit and carbohydrates.

However, even within our traditional diets, problems which are genetic, caused by over-indulgence or other physical problems and dietary imbalances, can be corrected by a change of diet for a period and then by a regular maintenance diet, which is created specially for the needs of different constitutions.

The advice for the more sedentary urban dweller is that the morning should begin with an intake of water and juice. Breakfast should be confined to fruits. Tea and coffee should be avoided as far as possible and for the diabetic, a brew made from roasted and coarsely pounded fenugreek seeds is essential. Those who are on a diet could take fresh herbal tea. Till lunch-time it should be just an intake of fruits or vegetables; cereals and proteins should be avoided.

Lunch can be a simple vegetarian meal with vegetables and wholewheat chapattis or handpounded rice and pickle.

A cup of tea in the late afternoon can be had, brewed in a pot and not boiled, with a dash of milk and brown sugar. Herbal tea is of course more advisable.

Dinner can be heavier, but should not be eaten too late. If you are eating proteins, they should be only twenty-five per cent of the food on your plate and the remaining food should be vegetables, salads with a judicious use of spices.

For people with certain basic problems such as a weak and sensitive digestive system, tendency towards obesity and resultant high blood pressure, respiratory difficulties, diabetes, or arteriosclerosis, the appropriate diet needs to be followed.

The basic dos and don'ts are actually quite simple. White flour, refined sugar, polished rice, processed food and aerated drinks are to be avoided. Everything in moderation, which includes alcoholic drinks. Protein in large quantities should be avoided. If a meal is heavy in protein and is not just a ladle of thin lentil sauce, then all forms of carbohydrates, including beer and ale, should be avoided.

The Western style diet books divide food into alkaline and acidic and organize diets accordingly, which is an effective way of eating sensibly. However, the Ayurvedic system looks at different food having linkages with the tridoshas *Vata-Kafa-Pita*. The diets prescribed by Ayurveda for different conditions are as important as the medicines. The leitmotif of Ayurvedic treatment is that if you have a balanced diet, you do not need medicine. A balanced diet will balance the *Vata-Kafa-Pita* for the body's internal chemistry to function in harmony. There are certain types of food which combine the requirements of all the three elements and are suitable for all conditions. These are wholewheat flour, old rice, green vegetables, ash gourd, potato, papaya, bel, apple, pomegranate, mango, melon, custard apple, ber, pineapple, guava, garlic, ginger and green chilli.

Vata or *vayu*, which is associated with the element of air, is the strongest element in our body. It moves through the body and can thus affect not only the joints but also the circulatory and nervous system. In fact, it is all pervasive and controls the five *prana*. The only way to control *vayu* is by introducing a certain amount of fat—*chiknai*—with the use of clarified butter, ghee. A teaspoon of clarified butter taken with rice, chapatti, or added to cooked food, or 2 tsp of butter per day is recommended. The dominance of *vata* is associated with restlessness, which in Hindi means *chanchal*, a vivacious mind but that which lacks concentration. The food to be avoided is an excess of new white rice, fibrous vegetables such as beans, okra, cabbage, radish and red meat as they will result in problems related to an imbalance of the *vayu*. The ideal diet for those who have an inner chemistry of *vayu* as one of the dominant elements should be old rice, wholewheat flour, moong dal, bottle gourd and vegetables of that family, snake gourd, tinda, touri, parwal, pumpkin, yellow and white petha, and aubergine. Bitter vegetables like karela or bitter gourd and fenugreek leaves or methi are very good and are recommended specially during the hot and humid season. Among the spicy elements, garlic and ginger form an essential part of the food along with green chillies. In the category of fruits, mangoes, pomegranate and apple are the best. Milk and curd should be taken in moderation, whereas buttermilk is the best and is known as food fit for the gods—*takra*.

Bhel/bel—*aeglo marmelos*—also known as Bengal quince, is not only rich in Vitamin C, but is an important cure for a number of digestive disorders. The bel can be eaten straight from the fruit after cracking it open. It can be mixed with water and shakkar, unrefined sugar, and made into a cooling sherbet. The dried bael fruit can be powdered and made into a sherbet, strained and drunk, and is known to cure chronic stomach disorders. Bel leaves grow in bunches of threes and are offered to Shiva. Ten to fifteen bel leaves made into a paste and taken with one cup of water, early in the morning for forty days, is supposed to be an effective cure for diabetes mellitus.

Kafa, which is often interpreted as phlegm, is associated with the element of water. Its role is that of a lubricator of the system. It gives lustre to the skin. A balanced *kafa* is visible in the relaxed bearing of people who are not stressed out and whose skin glows. There is a certain heaviness and slowness about the people in whom *kafa* dominates, yet they are capable of hard work, have good stamina, an ability to concentrate and are capable of in-depth research and study. They are of a calm temperament and slow to react.

An imbalance of *kafa* causes obesity, water retention and attendant problems, especially respiratory problems, as well as inflammation of the joints or the organs. Resultant infections are also common. Watermelon, urad ki dal, bananas, milk products and sweetmeats are to be avoided.

Pita translates as bile and is associated with the element of fire—*agni*. It controls the digestive metabolism as well as the optical system. The association of the light in the eyes, *tejas* or even the word *prakash*, is very expressive of the characteristics of *pita*. A balanced *pita* is a sign of an alert mind, as well as an active and balanced functioning of the liver, a connection that is not made by the allopathic system of medicine. Those with a dominance of *pita* are generally slim, have an alert mind and possibly an irritable nature. Their skin tends to be oily.

Pungent and bitter food activates the *pita*. Bitter vegetables, bitter gourd/karela, fenugreek leaves, methi, freshly budding leaves of margosa, neem roasted on a griddle with a touch of oil, garlic and ginger are advised, and so are green chillies or a dash of dry chillies. Tamarind and vinegar help the digestion, improve liver secretions and are good for the digestive system. Tamarind is also supposed to lower male libido, but the seeds of tamarind ground into a paste are, paradoxically, the cheapest form of aphrodisiac.

The mono diet where one type of fruit or vegetable is taken for forty days is known as the *kalpa* or rejuvenation diet which completely renews the intestinal system. This used to be part of the old system of fasting which was known as Chandrayan vrat and lasted for forty days, similar to the fasting for Lent by the Christians and by the Muslims for the month of Ramzan. The only difference was that the quantity of food was also regulated in the Chandrayan vrat. The rules of the Ethiopian Coptic Church for fasting for Lent are much stricter. During Lent those who fast only eat vegetables and pulses and refrain from eating even milk products. The Ethiopians practically stop work since they are prone to fainting spells as a result of this strict fast. It used to amuse me greatly and I would tease them by saying that what they consider fasting is the average diet of nearly eighty per cent of Indians.

Today, when we indulge ourselves frequently, partake of food and fruits which are out of season or are grown under different geo-climatical conditions, periodic fasting should be an essential part of our dietary pattern.

There are no hard and fast rules about diets for different types of metabolisms and resulting temperaments. A person may have a combination of two *doshas* and in some case even have all the three *doshas* making up their metabolism. Different types of systems demand different types of diet. It is advisable to consult a practitioner of Ayurveda who can identify which elements are the strongest in an individual's system and what they should avoid and what would be most beneficial for them. The importance of this book is that the recipes given in the

book cover all those vegetables which are generally
prescribed by the Ayurvedic system.

c e l e b r a t i o n   o f
f o o d

I generally plan the menu for a gathering based on the season and the tastes of those who are invited. If it is summer, then cold soup, salads, a hot dish and a light dessert are ideal. During the monsoon, a warm soup and cooked vegetables are more suitable for the palate and the digestive system. During this season, food should be light for this is the time when a number of gastric infections or problems of indigestion can occur. Winter is the time when a hot soup can give warmth and cooked food dominates the table, and one can then indulge a little and pamper oneself.

While planning a meal, attention has to be paid to every

detail. First, the aromas emanating from a piping hot dish, if possible freshly tempered. The next is the visual appeal. A rich range of colours adds warmth not only to the table but also to the mood of the company. Of course, the most important is the taste, the flavours and textures of the food.

I am giving a few examples to indicate how to plan your menus. There is a rich range of recipes to choose from.

SUMMER MENUS:
MENU 1
Cucumber and Curd Soup
Sesame and Beans Salad
Cucumber and Peanuts Salad
Pasta with Pesto Sauce
Mango Delight

The curd soup with cucumbers and mint is cooling. While the curd is white, the flecks of green mint along with the brown raisins add colour, texture and variation in taste. Walnuts satisfy the need to bite on something crunchy.

The beans salad with sesame is light, while the jade green cucumbers with peanuts look fresh, appetizing and add a hint of crunchiness to the salad.

The pasta with pesto sauce is light yet filling.

The mango delight rounds up the meal with the fruit of the season.

MENU 2
Pureed Delight: Ghia soup
Grilled tomatoes
Tindola salad
Crusty Valley: Pumpkin and Greens

For dessert, fresh fruit salad or small green melons cut in one-third and served with a scoop of ice-cream are ideal.

Here you have a medley of colours—jade green soup, red tomatoes, the mixed colours of the salad and golden yellow pumpkin and with dark green spinach.

This can be eaten with bread or wholewheat naan or chapatti.

WINTER MENUS:
MENU 1
> Kala Chana Soup Au Gratin
> Rembrandt's Dish: Aubergine with Mixed Vegetables
> Celery Delight
> Green Salad with rings of onion and fresh mushrooms
> Figs with Cream

A hearty soup takes the chill out of the bones and the mixed vegetables with the aubergine not only looks beautiful but is satisfying. The fresh light green celery is crisp and tasty. You could serve brown rice with the food. The figs with cream make a good dessert for the winter.

MENU 2
> Khatte wala Saag soup
> Pulao Fresh Peas
> Onion, Tomatoes and Paneer
> Gaajar Methi: Carrots and Dried Fenugreek
> Mixed Kachumbar salad
> Apricot Delight

A hot, sour and warming soup with a pale yellow base and dark green vegetables provide a contrast in colour with rich-glazed whole onions and red tomatoes. The orange carrot dish with flecks of black-green makes a medley of colours, tastes, flavours and aroma.

To be eaten with brown rice, or wholewheat chapattis.

MONSOON MENUS:

This is the time when you must be very careful with your diet. Do not use leftovers even if they are refrigerated. See that each day you have some bitter tasting vegetable at the beginning of your meal. Use garlic in the cooking and have, in addition, garlic chutney with each meal.

MENU 1

Golden Soup: Pumpkin Soup
Alu Methi: Potatoes and Fenugreek
Baingan Bhartha
Kumaoni Alu Tariwale
Mango Delight
Eat with wholewheat chapatti or pita bread.

MENU 2

Mixed vegetable soup
Karela sautéed
Kachi Pakki: Stir-Fried Cabbage
Pumpkin with Sour Plums and Spinach
Ghia Kofta Curry
Garlic Chutney
Petha Payasam
Eat with boiled rice.

These are just sample menus to indicate what goes together, using seasonal vegetables as well as what is good for different weather conditions.

It is good to start with a soup for it is healthy and filling.

You consume a good quantity of pure vegetables. It is also expedient when you have a party to keep your guests occupied while putting the final finishing touches and serving the food on the table.

It is always very disconcerting to have guests trooping into the kitchen and offering to help. I think the guest code should be to offer help, but wait to be asked to come and help. Do not start tasting food before it comes to the table. Another rule is to not ask for the recipe until the meal is over and your host/hostess is relaxed and you have a paper and pen in your hand. I find it most trying when people start asking for the recipe even before they have really tasted the food.

The way you serve the food is of utmost importance. Lay the dishes in such a way as to enhance their appearance. The bright yellow of lentil or pumpkin should be heightened by being served in a dark dish and being placed next to a darker green, as should be the orange of carrots and the red of the tomatoes. The first thing which announces the food is the aroma, so do the tempering just before serving. The next is the visual aspect, thus food served in appropriate containers, which augment the colour and show off the texture should be selected. The dishes should be placed with an eye to contrast or colour accents. I have seen an excellent meal served without care in presentation and thus losing the full impact of its qualities. And finally, of course, the acid test lies in the taste and the texture.

Glossary

Abbreviations used:
H—Hindi; Per—Persian; Pun—Punjabi; Guj—Gujarati;
U—Urdu; Ben—Bengali; Ara—Arabic; M—Marathi;
S—Sanskrit

Aata (H)	Wholewheat flour
Abgosht (Per)	Steamed meat cooked with potatoes chickpeas, spices and water
Ab-narang (Per)	Orange-flower water
Adas (Per)	Egyptian lentils (masoor dal)
Adrak (H)	Ginger
Ajmood	Parsley
Ajwain (H)	Bishop's weed

Ajwain patta (H)	Thyme
Akhrot (H)	Walnut
Alu (H)	Potato
Alu bukhara (H)	Dried sour plums
Amchur (H)	Sour dried mango powder
Anardana (H)	Dried pomegranate seeds
Anjeer (H)	Fig
Arabi (H)	Colocassia
Arhar dal (H)	Pigeon peas
Ash (Per)	Soup
Aspanak (Per)	Spinach
Badam (H)	Almond
Badi elaichi (H)	Black cardamom
Bagali kotak (Per)	A vegetable dish made of broad beans and herbs
Baingan (H)	Aubergine
Batata (Kanarese)	Potato
Besan (H)	Chickpea flour
Bhindi (H)	Okra
Burghul	Broken wheat
Chaana pani	Whey
Chaanch (H)	Buttermilk
Chaat (H)	Savoury snack
Chana dal (H)	Bengal gram
Chelo kabab (Per)	Rice with kabab

Chulie (H)	Amaranth
Dahi (H)	Curd
Dalchini (H)	Cinnamon
Dhania (H)	Coriander
Fitt-fiit (Amahra)	An instant dish made with a combination of dry injera and soup
Fufu (Per)	A gruel made from cassava, a staple food in West Africa
Gandho raj (Ben)	Lime tree with highly fragrant leaves
Gavar ki phali (H)	Cluster beans
Ghee (H)	Clarified butter
Guchi (Per)	Dried mushrooms/morrel
Gulab-arak (Urdu)	Rosewater
Gur (H)	Jaggery
Haldi (H)	Turmeric
Hara piaz (H)	Spring onion
Harissa (Ara)	Paste of red hot chillies used in Tunisia
Hing (H)	Asafoetida
Imli (H)	Tamarind
Jaiphal (H)	Nutmeg
Jeera (H)	Cumin
Jhinge (H)	Ridge gourd/touri
Kabab (H)	Spit-roasted meat

Kabuli chana (H)	White chickpeas
Kaddu (H)	Pumpkin
Kadipatta (H)	Curry leaf
Kaju (H)	Cashew nut
Kakari/kheera (H)	Cucumber
Kala chana (H)	Black chickpeas
Kala namak (H)	Rock salt
Kali mirch (H)	Peppercorn
Kalonji (H)	Onion seeds
Kashk (Per)	Dried whey
Kasuri methi (H)	Dried fenugreek leaves with a sharp taste and fragrance
Kathal (H)	Jackfruit
Keema (U)	Mince meat
Ker (H)	A berry of the desert
Kesar (H)	Saffron
Khoresthe kaddu (Per)	Pumpkin cooked with herbs and meat
Khum (Pun)	Mushrooms
Khurmani (H)	Apricot
Khus-khus (H)	Poppy seeds
Kimchee (Korean)	Pickled and fermented cabbage
Kishmish (H)	Raisin
Kitfoo (Amahra)	Raw minced beef served with hot butter melted with rosemary. A speciality of the Gurgee community of Ethiopia

Kochao/kocho (Amahra)	An extract from insett, the false banana grown by the Gurgee community in Ethiopia
Kofta (U)	Minced meat balls, also minced vegetables made into balls
Kokam (M)	*Garania indica*
Kukeh-sarah (Per)	A dish made of flour, eggs, and herbs gathered from the fields
Lahsan (H)	Garlic
Lal mirch (H)	Red chilli
Lavang (H)	Cloves
Leemu Ommani (Per)	Dried lime
Lobia (H)	Black-eyed beans
Louki (H)	Bottle gourd
Makkai (H)	Maize
Malai (H)	Thickened cream from the top of milk simmered over a period
Masoor dal (H)	Egyptian lentils
Matar (H)	Green peas
Matha (Pun)	Mixture of curd and water
Methi (H)	Fenugreek
Mooli (H)	Radish
Moong dal (H)	Green gram
Munakka (H)	Sultana
Murabba bahar narange (Per)	Jam made of orange flowers

Naan-e-barbari (Per)	Long flat bread made from white flour prepared with yeast and baked in a clay oven
Naan-e-sangark (Per)	Long flat bread made from wholewheat flour cooked on hot stones in an oven
Nam prik (Thai)	Chilli sauce
Narial (H)	Coconut
Paalak (H)	Spinach
Panch phoron (Ben)	Blend of five whole spices used in Bengali cuisine
Paneer (H)	Cottage cheese
Paneer-eh khushk (Per)	Dried sheep's cheese
Papad (H)	Fried or roasted crisp flat bread, made from powdered lentils
Parat (H)	A flat brass tray with raised sides for kneading dough
Parmal (H)	Wax gourd
Petha (H)	Ash gourd
Piaz (H)	Onion
Pista (H)	Pistachio
Poshto (Ben)	Poppy seeds
Poshto dhanush (Ben)	Okra cooked with poppy seeds
Pudina (H)	Mint
Rabri (H)	Sweetened milk thickened over a slow fire

Rai (H)	Mustard
Raita (H)	Curd mixed with vegetables
Rajmah (H)	Red kidney beans
Ras malai (Ben)	A milk and cottage cheese dessert
Sabut (H)	Whole
Sabzi khordan (Per)	Green herbs eaten uncooked with food
Sojani ki phalli (H)	Drumstick
Sarson ka tel (H)	Mustard oil
Saunf (H)	Aniseed
Shakkar (H)	Brown sugar
Shambalele (Per)	Fenugreek leaves
Shukto (Ben)	Dried vegetable with a bitter taste
Singhara (H)	Water chestnut
Soumak (Per)	A grainy sour herb served powdered with rice
Sounth (H)	Dried ginger powder
Surati papardi (Guj)	Cluster beans grown in Gujarat
Tandoor (H)	Clay oven for making roti/chapatti by slapping them to the heated wall. Also used for grilling
Tandoori (H)	Cooked in a clay oven
Tariwala/ taridar (H)	Curried vegetables
Tej patta (H)	Bay leaf
Tikia (H)	Cutlet

Til (H)	Sesame seeds
Tinda (H)	Small round vegetable of the bottle gourd family
Tindola (H)	A vegetable of the gourd family, resembling gherkin
Toor dal (H)	Pigeon peas
Touk (Ben)	Sour and sweet
Touri (H)	Ridge gourd
Toursh (Per)	Sour
Tulsi (H)	Basil
Urad dal (H)	Black gram
Vatinganah (S)	Aubergine

Index

988. If all the gold in the seas and oceans was mined and distributed to every person living on the planet, you would be the owner of 20 kg of gold!

989. Do you know that fire spreads faster uphill than downhill?

990. Do you know how many chemicals there are in a cigarette? Nearly 4000 of them, out of which more than 60 can cause cancer!

991. Imagine finding king cobras under your seat while travelling! Well, this happened in a train in Vietnam when the owner carried four bags weighing nearly 100 pounds, containing the writhing snakes, and placed them below the seat. The snakes were alive, but their mouths were shut and stitched. They were most probably on their way to Hanoi, since snake meat is considered a delicacy in Vietnam.

992. The Japanese live longer than any other people in the world. It's because of their healthy diet.

993. Canfield High School had a very special set of graduates in the class of 2011. Among the students, there were 10 sets of twins and a set of triplets. All of them had studied together right from kindergarten!

994. Harrods, in London, has the most the expensive pair of shoes in the world. Woven with platinum thread and embellished with about 640 rubies, these shoes easily cost more than $1.5 million.

995. What is the shape of a raindrop? Most of us seem to think that it resembles a teardrop. But scientists have captured images of raindrops using high-speed cameras and found that they look like hamburger buns!

996. What is the probability of people living for more than 116 years? With the current life expectancy levels, it is estimated to be just one in 2 billion!

997. Vietnam is shaped like the letter 'S'.

975. The Crayola crayon colour 'Prussian blue' was renamed 'midnight blue' in 1958. Apparently, kids couldn't relate to Prussian history, so teachers requested this change.

976. The first ever Olympic Games were held to honour the Greek king of gods, Zeus.

977. Russia, the largest country in the world, spans 11 time zones!

978. War is in the wind! Do you know that around 2500 collisions take place between birds and aircrafts every year in the US?

979. New Zealand was the first country in the world to give women the right to vote.

980. Silver was the most popular colour for cars in North America in 2002.

981. The Australian 50 cent coin has 12 sides to it!

982. Did you know that the average eyebrow has around 500 hairs?

983. In the years 1995 and 1996 Australia issued several stamps that looked just like gems.

984. The next time you install a doorknob, go for copper or brass ones instead of aluminium or steel. These metals disinfect themselves naturally and hence, spread lesser germs!

985. Try this out the next time you hear a cricket chirping! Count how many times the cricket chirps within 15 seconds, now add 40 to that number and you will have approximately calculated the temperature outside in Fahrenheit!

986. Have you ever wondered why the Mexican sombrero hat is so wide? It is meant to provide shade to the entire body!

987. If you arrange the population of China in a single file, you would probably never reach the end in your lifetime. Such is the rate of reproduction in the country!